From the author of *The Most Dangerous Book in the World:*
9/11 as Mass Ritual and *Most Dangerous: A True Story*

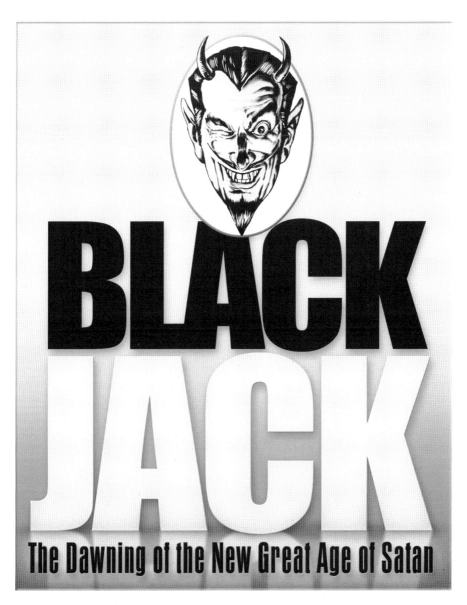

BLACK
JACK

The Dawning of the New Great Age of Satan

S.K. Bain

Published by:
Trine Day LLC
PO Box 577
Walterville, OR 97489
1-800-556-2012
www.TrineDay.com
publisher@TrineDay.net

Library of Congress Control Number: 2019941826

Bain, S. K.
Black Jack: The Dawning of the Great Age of Satan—1st ed.
p. cm.

Epud (ISBN-13) 978-1-63424-257-8
Mobi (ISBN-13) 978-1-63424-258-5
PDF (ISBN-13) 978-1-63424-252-3
Print (ISBN-13) 978-1-63424-256-1
1. Satanism 2. Psychological warfare -- United States -- History -- 21st century.
3. Occultism -- Political aspects -- United States.4. Secret societies -- United
States. 5. Conspiracies -- United States. 6. Political corruption -- United States.
I. Bain, S. K.. II. Title

FIRST EDITION
10 9 8 7 6 5 4 3 2 1

Printed in Korea by Four Clour Print Group, Louisville, Kentucky.

Distribution to the Trade by:
Independent Publishers Group (IPG)
814 North Franklin Street
Chicago, Illinois 60610
312.337.0747
www.ipgbook.com

Publisher's Foreword

Tao gives birth to One,
One gives birth to Two,
The Two gives birth to Three,
The Three gives birth to all universal things.
All universal things shoulder the Yin and embrace the Yang.
The Yin and Yang mingle and mix with each other to beget the harmony.
— Tao Te Ching

New beginnings are often disguised as painful endings.
— Attributed to Lao Tze

Therefore, stay awake, for you do not know on what day your Lord is coming. But know this, that if the master of the house had known in what part of the night the thief was coming, he would have stayed awake and would not have let his house be broken into. Therefore you also must be ready, for the Son of Man is coming at an hour you do not expect.
—Matthew 24:42-44

How did we get to here? Is it as black and white as some would like us to believe? What's next?

This book delves into the shadows of our lives, the underlining of our existence: the reality of the sacred … and the profane.

Most tenets boil down to two elixirs: predestination or free-will. What will be will be is easy to follow: you do nothing – enjoy the ride and maybe dip in a oar to help propel your fate. Free-will takes a bit more work, it demands action, serendipity, fortitude and a readiness to work with others.

What is America? To me, at its core, it is governance from the bottom up. And it is quite obvious that there are those that wish to impose governance from the top down. Will "they" succeed? Will the grand experiment, The United States of America, simply be a slight detour from rule by a few?

Secret societies have always been with us … and always will be: working to manipulate the narrative from prologue to epilogue. I have taken to heart the words of President Kennedy, "The very word 'secrecy' is repugnant in a free and open society; and we are as a people inherently and historically opposed to secret societies, to secret oaths, and to secret proceedings." I have also come to understand that a secret society is a thing – and like all things, it is not inherently good or evil, it is what the people involved make it. It is the action. *For every tree is known by its own fruit …*

Our country *did* arise from secret meetings, secret oaths and secret societies, because there have been times when good men have had to bind themselves in the shadows to fight against a worldly "evil" dominating their lives. Our forefathers worked to bring the dream of "life, liberty and the pursuit if happiness" to fruit. Kennedy's "free and open society" is but a twig of that tree – unfinished business of our imperfect union.

So much has changed. As time rolls by, will we go foreword in union, divide by design, or possibly regress into chaos by *con-fusion*? Read *BLACK JACK* by S.K. Bain and be forewarned!

Sacred geometry is neither good nor evil – it simply is: an attribute of existence. Some will use people's fears and fascinations as a divisive dialectic. Continuing an effort at "separation" that President Washington noted to Reverend G. W. Snyder in October, 1798:

> "It was not my intention to doubt that, the Doctrines of the Illuminati … had not spread in the United States. On the contrary, no one is more fully satisfied of this fact than I am.
>
> "The idea I meant to convey, was, that I did not believe that the Lodges of Free Masons in this Country had, as Societies, endeavoured to propagate the diabolical tenets…. That Individuals of them may have … actually had a separation of the People from their Government in view, is too evident to be questioned.

Be aware! We always have a choice, the question: what will we do?

Onward to the Utmost of Futures!

Peace,
R.A. Kris Millegan
Publisher
TrineDay
5/1/2019

Contents

INTRODUCTION

This is not so much an introduction as it is a prefacing comment. I am fully aware that there is a significant difference between the person of Satan and that of Lucifer, and between Satanism and Luciferianism. Before proceeding, however, I would merely point out that these two groups have a lot more in common with each other than they do with, say, Christianity.

Satan is, in a sense, a parody of Lucifer. That of course does not mean that Satanism is harmless. There are obviously hardcore worshippers of Satan who take their faith very seriously, and we should not fall for the overly-simplistic stereotype of Satanists in the popular culture.

I refer almost exclusively to Satan in this work, primarily for the sake of consistency. I do understand that the global elite are largely Luciferians, that the One-World Religion is Luciferianism, and that we all worship, willingly or unwillingly, knowingly or unknowingly, at the feet of the Light Bearer, for the entire world has become his temple. Many public ceremonies and events are now only thinly-veiled, if at all, public rituals, broadcast for all the nations to see.

As for the book itself, well, good luck.

I know that's Shiva on the left.

Thanks, guys, we've gotten the point already.

"This is not simply entertainment."

CHAPTER ONE

PROJECT BLACKJACK

June 22nd, the day after summer solstice. The world media is filled with horrifying coverage of near-simultaneous nuclear detonations in multiple major cities around the world: London, New York City, Washington, DC, Toronto, Mexico City, Portland, and Los Angeles. Hundreds of thousands of dead and dying. Property damage in the trillions. The global economy on the brink of collapse.

A right-wing cult takes credit for the attacks, but it turns out that the organization is a cut-out for a shadowy New-World-Order group of elites bent on world domination, their sinister plot hinging on *nuclear* false-flag terrorism. They were almost successful in using the ensuing global chaos to further their powerful grip on the nations of the earth, but were thankfully exposed and defeated.

PURE FICTION

Obviously, the scenario above was not based on a real-life attack, but was rather the storyline of an unusual slideshow series published on the website of the *London Telegraph* in early 2009 entitled "Project Blackjack."

The series consisted of five parts which were posted sequentially over the course of several weeks. The first several slideshows were rather basic and clunky, but the quality of the presentations improved with each subsequent posting, as did the sophistication of the content to a certain degree. Various slides contained a variety of secret codes, including several in hexadecimal format.

The slideshow also contained a variety of occult symbols and references to well-known conspiracy theories, such as the Roswell incident and Majestic 12, ostensibly contributing elements to the plotline, but a number of them seemed incongruous.

The series spawned all sorts of speculation and new conspiracy theories at the time, but when the date in question passed uneventfully, the public's fears were calmed.

A CRUMMY COMMERCIAL?

The slideshow guided readers to a website which contained additional information, much of it cryptic in nature, and the general consensus was ultimately that the entire thing had been a clever marketing ploy for a creative enterprise that never quite fully materialized. Thus, in the end, it wasn't entirely clear what the point of it all had been.

Thankfully, "Project Blackjack" was harmless fiction and subsequently relegated to the dustbin of conspiracy-theory history – although, periodically, someone with nothing better to do dredges it up and attempts to breathe new life into it by pinning the plot to an upcoming date, with the predictable result being that these occasions, too, invariably come and go without consequence.

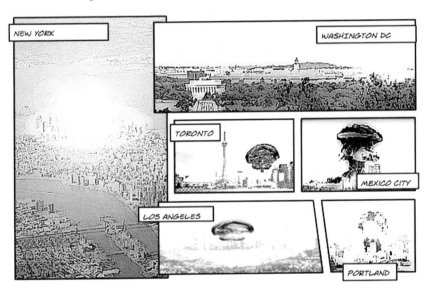

THE DAY AFTER

CHAPTER TWO

FALSE-FLAGS 101

There's terrorism, which has essentially been with us in one form or another since the Dawn of Man, and false-flag terrorism, which emerged nearly simultaneously with the first forms of government: Destroy something, blame it on those you dislike and unleash holy hell on them. More recently, the specter of nuclear terrorism has emerged, and, with it, the prospect of *nuclear* false flag terrorism.

NUCLEAR FALSE-FLAG TERRORISM

The horrendous reality of nuclear war has plagued the earth since Hiroshima and Nagasaki, and has been the subject of countless works of fiction and nonfiction, television programs and motion pictures. The possibility of state- or "shadow-government"-sponsored terrorism involving nuclear weapons is a fear that has manifested more recently and been dealt with in the media and popular culture to a lesser extent.

I wrote a fictitious scenario involving the latter in "Black Christmas: A Work of Predictive Fiction" (contained in *The Most Dangerous Book in the World: 9/11 as Mass Ritual*, published in 2012), which dealt with a Yuletide nuclear terror attack on Phoenix, Arizona, orchestrated by the global elite but, as on 9/11, carried out *by* and blamed *on* Muslim patsies. The attack was equal parts false flag terrorism, mass ritual and psychological warfare, just as were the real attacks of September 11, 2001.

ADVANCING THEIR CAUSE

Considering everything that the Cryptocracy accomplished through 9/11 and the ensuing aftermath – from the radical reduction in civil liberties to wars in Iraq and Afghanistan – one can only imagine that the global elite would very intentionally advance their interests across the board to an exponentially greater degree following an act of nuclear false-flag terrorism.

One could readily envision such an atrocity as being the pretext for a radical advancement of the vaunted New World Order, with its ever-progressing global technofascist police-state control grid and full spectrum dominance. Good thing that, to date, this particularly horrifying potentiality has remained in the realm of fiction.

CHAPTER THREE

THE END OF THE WORLD.
AGAIN.

While we're on the subject of scary stuff that never happened (or that at least hasn't happened *yet*), I'm sure that none of us have forgotten the much-hyped 2012 Mayan Apocalypse. The entire affair started off rather modestly with a small bunch of fruitcakes proclaiming that the end of the world was nigh, and by the time it was over everybody and their dog had jumped on the Bandwagon of Doom, including (not surprisingly) Hollywood and (only slightly surprisingly) the History Channel. A plethora of books, websites and documentaries – and well as a major motion picture – asserted that *this was it*, the Big One ... for real.

December 21st, 2012 was purported to be the end of the Mayan calendar and, according to ancient Mayan prophecy, the End of the World. But it was neither, and in fact the Mayans never said it would be. Their calendar did not end, and, obviously, neither did the world. In fact, as it turned out, that particular date was probably one of the slowest news days in modern history. (I don't think there was even a murder in Chicago that day.)

Funpocalypse

Well, there was at least *some* news on December 21st, 2012.

On this day, U.S. Senator and Skull & Bones member John Kerry was nominated by President Obama as the next Secretary of State, and the funeral service for long-time Democratic U.S. Senator from Hawaii Daniel Inouye was held at the National Cathedral in Washington, DC. For a variety of reasons I've speculated about elsewhere (2nd book, Chapter 50), I suspect that Inouye's timely passing and winter-solstice funeral constituted some sort of ritual-sacrifice-of-the-tribal-elder thing, but I'm not going to rehash that here.

A North Korean spokesperson once referred to U.S. Secretary of State John Kerry as a "wolf" with a "hideous lantern jaw." Previous creative insults hurled at American officials by representatives of the Hermit Kingdom included references to President Obama as "wicked black monkey" and a "crossbreed with unclear blood."

Arguably, the most significant event to occur that day, however, was the video for South Korean singer Psy's global mega-hit "Gangnam Style" hitting the unprecedented milestone of one billion views on YouTube.

Earlier in December 2012, a social media viral-marketing campaign was launched claiming that, according to one of Nostradamus' prophecies, Psy was in fact one of the Four Horsemen of the Apocalypse and that once his "Gangnam Style" YouTube video amassed a billion views, the world would come to an end. The campaign was a success, the goal was reached and everyone lived happily ever after.

Everyone, that is, except for reality television star couple Heidi Montag and Spencer Pratt, who, it was later revealed, had somewhat hastily spent most of their $10 million in accumulated earnings by 2010 because they actually believed the fictitious "Mayan Apocalypse prophecy" that the world would end in 2012..

Unsurprisingly, other (actual) celebrities with slightly more common sense successfully cashed in on the 2012 phenomenon, including Britney Spears with her hit "Till the World Ends."

See the sunlight, we ain't stopping
Keep on dancing till the world ends
If you feel it, let it happen
Keep on dancing till the world ends
Keep on dancing till the world ends
Keep on dancing till the world ends

Even Jello got in on the act. Funpocalypse…

DOOM WE CAN ALL BELIEVE IN

December 21st, 2012, *had* marked the end of a rather large block of time number of days on the Mayan calendar. It was the end of "13 baktun," 13 sets of 144,000 days, a total of 1,872,000 days – a Mayan "Age," not to be confused with a zodiacal age, which varies in length depending on which astrologer you're talking to. The Mayans, however, never said that this event would herald the destruction of the planet. No asteroids. No solar kill strike. No geomagnetic pole reversal. No alien invasion.

(Left) Scene from Mars Attacks. *In the background, the pyramidal Las Vegas Luxor Hotel, site of the October 1, 2017, Route 91 Festival massacre, the largest mass shooting in American history.*

The idea of the year 2012 as the End of All Things slowly gained momentum in the years preceding, and by the time the thing gained a full head of steam, it had turned into the biggest steaming pile of unsubstantiated pseudoscientific horse manure the world has ever seen. Hordes of the undiscerning jumped on board, zealously peddling boatloads of nonsensical conjecture regarding global cataclysmic effects that would result from this, that and the other, and proselytizing anybody who would listen.

It seemed for a time that practically everybody outside the mainstream scientific community had bought into the modern myth to some degree or another, and a genuine Apocalyptic fervor gripped large swaths of the planet. During the very finite window of time leading up to 2012, proponents and practitioners of almost every ethnic group and religion on earth breathlessly purported that, indeed, *their* prophecies, scriptures, elders and priests, too, spoke of this time in human history as being The End. *Don't tell us it's the bleeping end of the world, we knew it all along.*

MUCH ADO ABOUT NOTHING

Interestingly, the timing of the completion of 13 baktun coincided with a real-world event that came to be referred to as "Galactic Alignment," and a small group of non-mainstream Mayan scholars and researchers contended that this was indeed by design on the part of the Mayans.

Galactic Alignment is a purely visual phenomenon occurring from the perspective of the surface of the earth. Due to the wobble in the earth's axis and the resulting "precession of the equinoxes," every 26,000 years or so the sun, from our vantage point, lines up with the galactic equator near galactic center – more precisely in a region known as "the dark rift." In reality, this visual alignment didn't occur only on December 21ˢᵗ, 2012, but has taken place over a roughly 40-year period, beginning around 1976.

Nothing physically lines up with anything else in the galaxy; the earth doesn't pass through some precise magical magnetic centerline of the galactic equator and get sucked into the supermassive black hole at the heart of the Milky Way. There's no deadly burst of cosmic rays, no macro quantum effect, and the earth doesn't "move from its place" (Old Testament).

So what's the big deal if Mayan priests and astronomers, who kept very detailed and accurate astronomical records (What else did they have to do other than sit around and stare at the night sky anyway?), methodically worked out several hundred years in advance which heavenly features were going to be aligned with each other at some future date? Big whoop.

You mean to tell me all the fuss over 2012 was basically because some old South American shamans in antiquity stayed up way too late way too often drinking way too much DMT-laden ayahuasca and centuries later a handful of half-educated Western dipnuts mis-interpreted their glyphs as prophesying the End of Time … and half the population of the planet bought in?

I suppose the only silver lining in all of this is that, just like all the false warnings of nuclear false-flag terrorism, nothing came of it in the end.

FROM THE PRODUCER OF "PIRATES OF THE CARIBBEAN"
NICOLAS CAGE
A JERRY BRUCKHEIMER PRODUCTION
A JON TURTELTAUB FILM
NATIONAL TREASURE
MDCCLXXVI
IN ORDER TO BREAK THE CODE, ONE MAN WILL HAVE TO BREAK ALL THE RULES.
WALT DISNEY PICTURES PRESENTS IN ASSOCIATION WITH JERRY BRUCKHEIMER FILMS NICOLAS CAGE "NATIONAL TREASURE" A JUNCTION ENTERTAINMENT PRODUCTION IN ASSOCIATION WITH SATURN FILMS A JON TURTELTAUB FILM HARVEY KEITEL JON VOIGHT
DIANE KRUGER SEAN BEAN JUSTIN BARTHA AND CHRISTOPHER PLUMMER MUSIC SUPERVISOR BOB BADAMI MUSIC BY TREVOR RABIN COSTUME DESIGNER JUDIANNA MAKOVSKY FILM EDITOR WILLIAM GOLDENBERG, A.C.E. PRODUCTION DESIGNER NORRIS SPENCER DIRECTOR OF PHOTOGRAPHY CALEB DESCHANEL
EXECUTIVE PRODUCERS MIKE STENSON CHAD OMAN CHRISTINA STEINBERG BARRY WALDMAN OREN AVIV CHARLES SEGARS PRODUCED BY JERRY BRUCKHEIMER JON TURTELTAUB STORY BY JIM KOUF SCREENPLAY BY TED ELLIOTT & TERRY ROSSIO AND MARIANNE WIBBERLEY & CORMAC WIBBERLEY
DIRECTED BY JON TURTELTAUB
11.19.04
nationaltreasure.com
JERRY BRUCKHEIMER FILMS
Walt Disney Pictures

CHAPTER FOUR

MONUMENTAL SPECULATION

The U.S. Capitol building. The Washington Monument. The Lincoln Memorial. The White House. The incredible architecture and monuments of our nation's capital became everyday sights for me when I worked in Washington, DC, from 1995-2001. They never fail to impress when you look at them, but those who live and work there notice them less and less over time.

Lots of conspiracy theorists have ideas about what many of the building and monuments in DC symbolize. Major motion pictures such as *National Treasure* and best-selling books such as *The Lost Symbol* have effectively capitalized on such speculation.

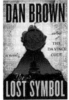

THE WRATH OF 'KHAN

Not long after I arrived in DC, leader of the Nation of Islam Louis Farrakhan organized "The Million Man March," and in his address to the attendees in the capital that day, he made multiple references to symbols he claimed were incorporated in the layout of Washington, DC, and to related numerology. The whole event was somewhat of a spectacle, but the occult references in particular amused a number of the journalists at the then-newly-launched neoconservative *Weekly Standard* magazine where I served as art director.

Farrakhan spoke:

> There, in the middle of this mall is the Washington Monument, 555 feet high. But if we put a 1 in front of that 555 feet, we get 1555, the year that our first fathers landed on the shores of Jamestown, Virginia as slaves. In the background is the Jefferson and Lincoln Memorial, each one of these monuments is 19 feet high.
>
> Abraham Lincoln, the sixteenth president. Thomas Jefferson, the third president, and 16 and 3 make 19 again. What is so deep about this number 19? Why are we standing on the Capitol steps today? That number 19! When you have a nine, you have a womb that is pregnant. And when you have a one standing by the nine, it means that there's something secret that has to be unfolded. ...

Continuing:

> Well, the day that these presidents feared has now come to pass, for on this mall, here we stand in the capital of America, and the layout of this great city, laid out by a Black man, Benjamin Banneker. This is all placed and based in a secret Masonic ritual. And at the core of the secret of that ritual is the Black man. Not far from here is the White House.

> And the first president of this land, George Washington, who was a grand master of the Masonic order, laid the foundation, the cornerstone of this capitol building where we stand. George was a slave owner. George was a slave owner. Now, the President spoke today and he wanted to heal the great divide. But I respectfully suggest to the President, you did not dig deep enough at the malady that divides Black and White in order to affect a solution to the problem. And so, today, we have to deal with the root so that perhaps a healing can take place.

Now, this obelisk at the Washington Monument is Egyptian, and this whole layout is reminiscent of our great historic past, Egypt. And, if you look at the original Seal of the United States, published by the Department of State in 1909. Gaylord Hunt wrote that late in the afternoon of July 4, 1776, the Continental Congress resolved that Dr. Benjamin Franklin, Mr. John Adams, and Mr. Thomas Jefferson be a committee to prepare a device for a Seal of the United States of America. ...

The Seal and the Constitution reflect the thinking of the founding fathers, that this was to be a nation by White people and for White people. Native Americans, Blacks, and all other non-White people were to be the burden bearers for the real citizens of this nation.

For the back of the Seal, the committee suggested a picture of Pharaoh sitting in an open chariot with a crown on his head and a sword in his hand, passing through the divided waters of the Red Sea, in pursuit of the Israelites. And, hovering over the sea was to be shown a pillar of fire in a cloud, expressive of the divine presence and command.

And rays from this pillar of fire were to be shown, beaming down on Moses standing on the shore, extending his hand over the sea, causing it to overwhelm Pharaoh. The motto for the reverse was "Rebellion to Tyrants is Obedience to God." Let me say it again. Rebellion to tyrants is obedience to God.

Ultimately, whatever "secret that has to be unfolded" Farrakhan was referring to remained hidden, as nobody could figure out what in the hell he was talking about. Most members of the mainstream media simply ignored his occult references or considered them as essentially the ramblings of a race-baiting demagogue.

COMPLETE REVERSAL

At the time, I paid no attention to Farrakhan's cryptic references, nor was I in the least interested in conspiracy theories or alternative history. On one family outing to the National Mall, as I observed distant family relative Benjamin Franklin's signature, along with those of the other signers of the Declaration of Independence, etched in stone on Signers Island in Constitution Gardens, I had no idea of his purported connections with the infamous Hellfire Club or any of the other clandestine or unsavory activities that fringe researchers accuse him of being involved with.

(Left) Signers Island.

(Center) Members of the Irish Hellfire Club shown in a portrait by James Worsdale in the National Gallery of Ireland. (Right) Sir Francis Dashwood.

I suppose then that it is somewhat ironic that, over a decade later in 2012, the first of two books on conspiracy theories I authored was published. The first, as mentioned previously, is entitled *The Most Dangerous Book in the World: 9/11 as Mass Ritual*, and the second, *Most Dangerous: A True Story*, published in 2015, in part concern a series of unfortunate events that befell me and my family as a direct result of my authoring the first book.

The story of my transition from the mainstream media world to the bizarre conspiracy-theory alternate universe is not as interesting, or as tragic, as that of my transition from working in one of the most influential political magazines in the most powerful city in the world to becoming unemployed and living in a mobile home in my in-laws backyard in rural northeast Mississippi – but both of those subjects are a story for another time (if ever).

CHAPTER FIVE

THE BIG ONE

Although the 2012 Doomsday was a huge non-happening, Galactic Alignment was, in a sense, very real. It did not involve forces of nature or the supernatural run amok, and presented no physical danger to humanity. It did, however, involve the alignment of heavenly bodies and other features in the night sky (if only from our vantage point), which is to say, the stuff that astrology is made of.

If there ever was a genuine metaphysical science that the modern superstition of astrology might have descended from, as some current followers of the ancient Vedic tradition contend, then that particular brand of wisdom is lost to the sands of time, because what we're left with today is pure hocus pocus. Nonetheless, astrology remains an integral aspect of the contemporary occult mindset.

STAR STRUCK

So although Galactic Alignment itself presented no existential threat to humanity, there are those very powerful practitioners of the occult for whom this celestial phenomenon would have been quite significant – a once-in-a-26,000-year occasion. And among those practitioners are the super-elite psychopaths who rule the planet and control all its resources and peoples.

These privileged few are not simply the socio-economic elite, but are elite practitioners of the dark arts, as well, and they are particularly fond of timing their Satanic soirees to astrologically auspicious occasions in order to induce the dark powers to bless their evil undertakings.

As I chronicle in my previous books, the Cryptocracy time many, if not all, of their rituals and false flag attacks to coincide with important dates on the occult calendar, which is often when the moon or some planet is in a favorable orientation with another, or something along those lines.

For those who have not read my first book, such was the case with the attacks of September 11th, 2001: this date was selected with intentionality and great purpose, and is of great importance to worshipers of the Dog Star, Sirius, the Blazing Star of the Freemasons and the celestial abode of Lucifer.

THE MOTHER OF ALL AUSPICIOUS OCCASIONS

If, then, this practice of timing ill deeds by the motions and positions of heavenly bodies is indeed a foundational aspect of our masters' modus operandi, would they not have then marked Galactic Alignment in spectacular fashion? Indeed, they did.

As I detailed in *9/11 as Mass Ritual*, the dazzling elaborate hugely-expensive opening and closing ceremonies of the 2012 London 30th (XXX) Olympics were globally-televised mass rituals (minus the human sacrifice) marking the grand celestial alignment, esoterically symbolized by the Triple Cross (XXX)... mere months from the 12/21/12 Mayan Doomsday date.

The phoenix and a super-sized Lord Voldemort.

We should then, be thankful the psychopathic Luciferian global elite chose, for whatever reason(s), not to include the mass-human-sacrifice element in their in-plain-sight observance of the momentous 2012 Galactic Alignment, and that the danger presented by this Mother of All Auspicious Occasions is fully past... although, come to think of it, if you'll recall, Galactic Alignment was not confined to the year 2012...

AN
AMERICAN
HIROSHIMA

BY THE AUTHOR OF *SOLDIER X*
Don Wulffson

CHAPTER SIX

AN EVER-PRESENT DANGER

Speaking of dangers that have (hopefully) fully past, the ever-elusive 9/11 boogeyman Osama bin Laden, despite having the world's top intelligence agencies and elite military units tracking him for the better part of a decade, managed to single-handedly further traumatize and terrorize the United States populace from half a world away with threats of an "American Hiroshima" – a supposed planned attack on one or more major American cities using a nuclear device or radiological "dirty bomb."

According to the official narrative, OBL had already successfully attacked the homeland – and, now, he was poised to do so again with exponentially more devastating effect. Oh, the horror.

RED HOT TERROR

For decades we've faced the threat of annihilation from global thermonuclear war – Mutually Assured Destruction (or aliens) seems to have kept that at bay. Rogue nation-states such as Iran and North Korea also present an ever-present danger with regards to a nuclear attack and nuclear proliferation, although these bad geopolitical actors have also thus far been contained. Nuclear terrorism, on the other hand, a "kook with a nuke," has emerged as an amorphous threat of which the global public lives in perpetual fear. Effective deterrents for nuclear terror are far more complex and elusive.

If you need this explained to you, you probably shouldn't be reading this book.

As we all know from watching the historical documentary *Zero Dark Thirty*, the CIA-created former mujahideen warrior bin Laden was killed by Seal Team 6[1] in Pakistan, so there's no longer any need to worry about his American Hiroshima. Bin Laden, however, was merely the temporary face of this form of modern terror, which obviously survived his demise (whenever that may have occurred).

WORTH WORRYING ABOUT?

Exactly how much time, though, should we spend worrying about nuclear war with Russia or China, or a more limited nuclear attack by Iran or North Korea, or an American-Hiroshima-style terror attack? These are all among the unsettling possible realities of modern life. Should we worry about these eventualities any more than, say, a global pandemic?

The subtitle of The Dunces of Doomsday: *"10 blunders that gave rise to Radical Islam, Terrorist Regimes, and the threat of an American Hiroshima"*

Some scholars maintain that we remain as close, or have come even closer, to "nuclear midnight" than we were during the Cold War, but is this actually the case? There are obvious and powerful deterrents to attacks by other nations, and technologies for the detection of nuclear weapons and radiological materials such as might be utilized by terrorist groups have improved and proliferated dramatically in the last decade.

MEANS AND MOTIVE

Indeed, it would be wise to ask ourselves whether the *most pressing* threat of nuclear terrorism might instead be posed by those with the proven ability to manipulate the intelligence services and militaries of the world's most powerful countries, as occurred on 9/11 – those who have

---

1. If the official story of bin Laden's assassination were false in any respect, wouldn't at least some of the members of Seal Team 6 reportedly involved in the raid have publicly disputed it, or threatened to? Google "Extortion 17." Oh, and try to find a photo of bin Laden being buried at sea, which the Pentagon claimed was Islamic tradition, but isn't.

demonstrated the capacity and willingness to slaughter innocent civilians to advance their own nefarious causes?

Keep in mind that false flag attacks are not necessarily carried out by governments themselves, but frequently by shadow forces operating deep within its structures, manipulating it unseen. Sorry all you Bush haters... if you still think W. had the sense to pull off 9/11 by himself, you need to do your homework.

Multiple choice: If Osama bin Laden and his 9/11 co-conspirators were CIA/shadow-government-created radical Muslim fall guys, that would make the terrible events of September 11, 2001:

1. A birthday party.

2. Cheese dip.

3. A false flag attack.

For the correct answer, turn the book over and hit yourself in the head with it.

CHAPTER SEVEN

WHEEL IN THE SKY

T he ancient Maya were by no means the only civilization interested in Galactic Alignment, or the only peoples of antiquity who
looked forward into the future towards this momentous event.

To fully understand the strong interest in this astronomical phenomenon requires a great deal of background research and if, unlike myself,
you have not devoted a considerable (and perhaps questionable) amount
of time to this task and aren't fully versed in the subject matter, I'll try to
make this as brief as possible.

Fully accounting for the near-universal presence of the Zodiac dating
back millennia in the many diverse cultures of the world, separated by
vast amounts of time and geography, is a considerable task. The Zodiac
plays an integral role in the identities and myth-making of a broad range
of civilizations across eons.

Wheel of the zodiac: This 6th century mosaic pavement in a synagogue incorporates Greek-Byzan-
tine elements, Beit Alpha, Israel. The zodiac signs in a 16th-century woodcut.

Why would this be so? The Zodiac has since time immemorial aid-
ed man in tracking the path of the sun through the sky on its annual cir-
cuit through the heavens. It has also performed a much less well-known
purpose, one that was/is at the core of many mystery religions, and this
esoteric knowledge was among the most closely guarded secrets of these
hidden wisdom traditions.

In addition to its annual 'timekeeping' function, the Zodiac is also a
Precessional Clock that allows us to track the passage of long stretches of
time. As the earth wobbles slowly on its axis, the axis traces out a circle in

the heavens, passing through all the signs of the Zodiac before returning to its starting position.

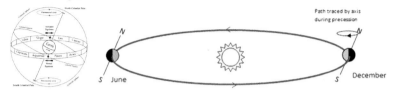

This process of the great "Wheel in the Sky" going through one full rotation takes approximately 26,000 years. The Eternal Wisdom regards this "Great Age" and the beginning and ending of this repeating grand cycle. The end of one cycle marks the start of the next: that moment in time is the Alpha and the Omega.

IT AIN'T OVER 'TIL ...

The end of a Mayan age on December 21st, 2012, was more precisely held to be the completion of the *fifth* age on their calendar, each of these ages lasting approximately 5,125 years. Five of these ages would last roughly 26,000 years – or about the length of a Great Age.

Was the end of the Mayan Fifth Age also the end of the Great Age, and how do we know when the Precessional Clock starts and stops? Recall from an earlier chapter that during Galactic Alignment "the sun, from our vantage point, lines up with the galactic equator near galactic center," and that this occurs once every 26,000 years.

Does Galactic Alignment, then, mark the Alpha and the Omega, the end of one Great Age and the beginning of the next – and, if so, was the completion of 13 baktun on the Mayan calendar (corresponding to December 21st, 2012, on the Gregorian calendar), the precise end date of the Great Age?

Yes and no. Galactic Alignment is the marker for the end of the Great Age, but it was not completed on 12/21/12. Recall from earlier discussion that the alignment is a transition that occurs over a roughly 40-year period beginning around 1976,[1] which means that it is not technically over until 2020-2021. Interesting.

So, the Mother of All Auspicious Occasions isn't over, and when it *is* over, and the end of the current Great Age is official, the new Great Age will begin, won't it?

The Great Age is referred to as the Great Year. We annually celebrate New Year's Eve/Day with fireworks around the globe. What do you think that the Cryptocracy would consider a fitting manner by which to celebrate New Great Year's Eve/Day and greet the New Great Age?

Project Blackjack, anyone?

More multiple choice: If the Cryptocracy staged nuclear terror attacks around the world and blamed them on another entity (wait, that sounds familiar), such as Iran, ISIS or North Korea, that would make these tragic events:

1. A birthday party.

2. Cheese dip.

3. A false flag attack.

For the correct answer, call (202) 456-1111.

1.The reason for this 40-year window is that the sun, being about ½ degree in width, takes about that long to pass through the imaginary Galactic Equator. (Remember, it's *all* imaginary.)

Hell on Earth

PHILIP PALMER

CHAPTER EIGHT

THE NEW GREAT AGE OF SATAN

To recap what we've covered thus far…

1. Nuclear *false flag* terrorism is an ever-present threat.

2. Coming up in the near future we have The Mother of All Auspicious Occasions in the Dawning of the New Great Age.

3. The world is run by a gaggle of insanely powerful psychopathic multi-generational Satanists who look for every opportunity to ritually sacrifice fellow human beings to their evil god.

4. The planetary power structure is primed for, and an extensive amount of groundwork has been laid for, an exponential leap forward into a full-blown technofascist global dictatorship – the *true* New World Order. We are one mass terror attack/mass sacrifice away from being plunged into the depths of tyranny. *How to Create a Prison Planet in One Easy Step.*

Now, it may just be me, but that sounds like a can't-miss recipe for hell on earth, or false-flag terror heaven, whichever way you want to look at it.

Really, if you think about it, what better way could you come up with to greet the New Great Age and properly commemorate this once-in-a-26,000-year event than to slaughter countless innocent men, women and children in a mass sacrificial nuclear holocaust in honor of your Dark Lord – thereby dedicating the new cosmic cycle as the New Great Age of Satan while simultaneously shifting the machinery of global tyranny into overdrive?

Sounds like a plan to me.

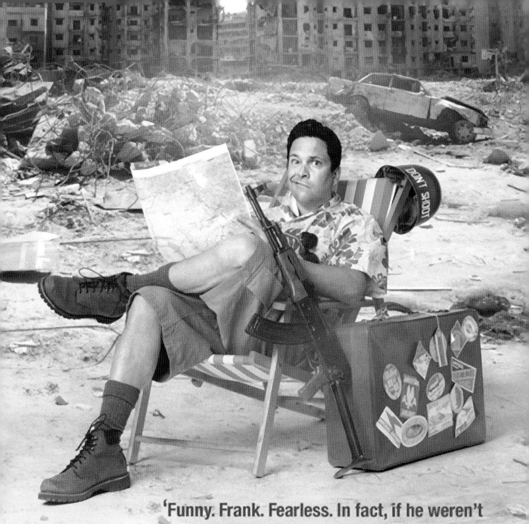

'Funny. Frank. Fearless. In fact, if he weren't
called Dom Joly, that would be a much better
name for him' DANNY WALLACE

THE DARK
TOURIST

**Sightseeing in the world's most unlikely
holiday destinations** DOM JOLY

CHAPTER NINE

A BAD TRIP

For the sake of argument, let's say that the Cryptocracy did have something like the scenario outlined in the last chapter in the works. Wouldn't they have left intentional clues all over the place – in-plain-sight clues for the initiated foretelling their intentions?

You can bet your ass they would have.

SYMBOLIC TRUTH

Author Michael Tsarion has observed that modern man suffers from "chronic symbol illiteracy" and that we will remain subject to mass manipulation until we become "lucidly cognizant and profoundly educated concerning the power of symbols."

In my first book, I discuss the importance of number and symbol to the practitioners of the occult. I quote author and mystic Manly P. Hall from *Lectures on Ancient Philosophy*, in which he states, "Symbols are oracular forms – mysterious patterns creating vortices in the substances of the invisible world. They are centers of a mighty force, figures pregnant with an awful power, which, when properly fashioned, loose fiery whirlwinds upon the earth."

I also quote Helena Petrovna Blavatsky, one of the founders of the Theosophical Society, from *Isis Unveiled*, in which she writes, "all systems of religious mysticism are based upon numerals." I quote other authorities on the metaphysical significance of number and symbol, as well, but you get the point.

HITTING THE HIGHLIGHTS

Numbers and symbols are part of a secret language that the elite use to communicate with each other in plain sight, right under our symbolically-illiterate noses. As with any foreign language with which we are unfamiliar, much of it would seem like gibberish even if we were to notice it.

One not only has to learn the meaning behind the individual components of the language, but also the grammar and syntax. *9/11 as Mass Ritual* deals with the "occult signature" of the event, the numbers and symbols employed that day, including the twin towers, the pentagon and the flight numbers of the planes involved. The book also discusses the astrology and numerology associated with this globally-televised black mass.

But if you want any more background than that on those subjects, I'd invite you to read the book, because: a.) I don't feel like repeating it all here; b.) we really have too much to cover to get into a lot of detail on all that right now; and, c.) I'm really a visual artist (art director, graphic designer), not a writer, and I'd rather show than tell.

In fact, it would be better if you thought of me as your tour guide. I know a little about a lot of things – I can show you the major attractions and tell you the basic facts, but if you want a lot of details, read up afterwards. It's far more important that we look at the big picture here and not get lost in the weeds. We're going to look rather briefly at each individual landmark, and then move on to the next one.

MAKING DO

There are certainly far more talented writers, much better educated researchers, infinitely smarter thinkers, and vastly more well-travelled guides than myself, but you're stuck with me, so we'll make the best of it.

The truth is that without necessarily realizing it, you've signed up for a "dark tourism" excursion through a horrifying landscape with a less-than-qualified tour guide. I'll do my best to get you out in one piece.

A FERNANDO MEIRELLES FILM

CITY OF GOD

STARRING
ALEXANDRE RODRIGUES, DOUGLAS SILVA,
AND LEANDRO FIRMINO.

OFFICIAL SELECTE

CHAPTER TEN

HOLY GROUND

Before we start scanning the environment and combing the landscape for clues, we need to have some idea what we're looking for, and this relates directly to the question, When? When, by the reckoning of the Cryptocracy (because their opinion is truly the only one that matters), is The End, and, by extension, The Beginning?

We know that the general answer to that question is, *Now*. More specifically, we are nearing the end of the 40-year window of Galactic Alignment and the year 2021 will mark its completion. A short couple of years away.

So, we look for encoded references to 2021 as the End of Days, the Apocalypse, etc.? Sort of. Where do you even start to look, though?[1]

GETTING POINTED IN THE RIGHT DIRECTION

In order to have an idea what to look for, we also need to further understand the symbology associated with Galactic Alignment. I've already mentioned the XXX London Olympics and the Triple Cross – the three symbolic crosses formed by: 1.) the plane of the ecliptic (path of the sun through the sky) and the galactic equator (the centerline of the visible band of the Milky Way), known as the Great Cross, and, 2.) the rotational axes and equators of the earth and sun – all three crosses align during Galactic Alignment.

There are two additional crosses to consider, as well (a second Triple Cross, if you will). In my first book, I explain:

> As the Gospels record, two criminals were crucified with Jesus, one
> on either side, thus the three crosses often associated with Chris-

---

1. You know the answer: right under our noses.

tianity. Astronomically, in addition to the Great Cross, there is: Cygnus (the Latinized Hellenic Greek word for swan), lying on the plane of the Milky Way, which contains the Northern Cross; and, Crux (Latin for cross), with contains the Southern Cross – both of which are in close proximity to Galactic Center and lay on either side of the Great Cross.

Compellingly, the Mayans also recognized two cross-shaped constellations in this same region (although they are not identical with Cygnus and Crux): "Xic," the Hawk (hawk, swan, whatever) and The Thieves' Cross (criminals, thieves, whatever) – both of which figured into Mayan myths focused on telling the unfolding story of the heavens, past, present and future.

Other associated symbols include the Zodiacal signs of Scorpio and Sagittarius, located on either side of Galactic Center. Scorpio's stinger and Sagittarius' arrow both point directly at the center of the Milky Way galaxy, which is often symbolized as a womb, as in the Womb of Creation, or skull (or skull cap); also, as a cosmic mountain or the throne of god.

(Left) Ball-player disc from Chinkultic, Chiapas. (Center) The ball-game court of Chichen Itzá. (Right) Stone hoop at Chichen Itzá.

AS ABOVE, SO BELOW

Many ancient cultures mapped the heavens onto the local landscape. Their great cities and monuments were built in a manner that reflected celestial features and the relationships of heavenly bodies. Kings were often viewed as manifestations or representatives of god, and often ruled from the City of God, an earthly counterpart of the heavenly City of God, which many times was held to be located at the center of what we know today is the Milky Way galaxy (and is, in fact, the most prominent feature in the night sky).

Some might find it surprising that this practice of mapping heaven to earth has continued into modern times – and even more surprising where these "astronomical encodings" can be found today.

HIDDEN CLUES

A very interesting related question is this: If the elements and symbols associated with "precessional cosmology" are encoded in the historic and contemporary landscapes and built environments, might not knowledge of the cycle of precession, and perhaps even Galactic Alignment, be found there, as well?

The short answer is, Yes. (The long answer constitutes a considerable portion of the remainder of this book. Read on.)

It was not uncommon to find a river flowing through these Cities of God that represented the Milky Way. Womb or birth imagery, symbolizing galactic center, was frequently utilized in various cultures. Myth-making often involved the use of precessional symbols and creatively told the unfolding story of the heavens and the turning of the Great Wheel in the Sky, which is completing yet another full turn in our era.

Architectural and artistic references to the Great Age are strikingly common, as are, to a lesser extent (if you know what to look for), encodings of the hidden wisdom regarding the End of the Great Age.

Having said all that, if at this point you still find all of this a little vague and are wondering where I'm going with it, don't worry – it'll become clear soon enough, and once it has, you'll wish it hadn't.

Alice
in Wonderland

CHAPTER ELEVEN

DOWN THE RABBIT HOLE

L ittle did I know it when I worked there, but Washington, DC, as I have since come to learn, is filled with esoteric imagery – as well as celestial alignments in the street layout and architecture – to the degree that it could almost be thought of as an Occult Wonderland. Louis Farrakhan was on to something, after all (this is not to imply by any means that the conclusions he drew in his Million Man March speech were correct).

As I researched and wrote about the attacks of 9/11 and related occult symbolism, the DC I knew so well took on an entirely new level of meaning. The Pentagon was of course one of the targets of the attacks, and the pentagon itself a powerful occult symbol – but, as it turns out, just one of many in the landscape of our nation's capital.

As I was to learn, the Washington Monument and Capitol Dome represent the phallus of Osiris and womb of Isis, but there is much, much more than I ever imagined in this place I thought I knew so well, including, as David Ovason points out in his book, *The Secret Architecture of Our Nation's Capital*, over twenty complete zodiacs.

(Right) Festive family portrait: (L-R) Johnny Depp dressed as the Mad Hatter as he joined Michelle, Malia, Barack and Sasha Obama in the White House.

HANG ON

Now, I could provide a ton of additional detail here, and on other related subjects throughout this book, but the truth is that you're either going to believe the case I'm making or you're not. Depending on your level of knowledge in the associated topics discussed herein, you're either going to have an existing knowledge base that will assist you in assessing my claims, or you're going to have to do additional reading – either way, you're still going to have to decide for yourself.

No matter how much I ramble on, or how many other authorities or authors I quote, or how many other books I cite, and no matter who or what you've read previously, you're either going to swallow this pill or spit it out.

So I'm not going to do a lot of additional setup. I'm going to throw it all out there and we're going to have fun on our little trip, even if it is through the devastated landscape of a possible future Apocalypse. You've bought your ticket, and now the ride really begins.

CHAPTER TWELVE

TICK-TOCK

The Cryptocracy's control of our planet and all its resources and peoples is complete, total, and it takes great pride in demonstrating this total mastery and flaunting it in our faces. (If you don't believe this statement, take this book and throw it in the garbage. Nothing else in it will make sense to you.)

The global elite engage in all sorts of wickedly humorous in-plain-sight, in-your face mockery of we, the useless eaters, a fact that I and others have written about extensively. As but one example, multiple aspects of the 9/11 Luciferian Megaritual were simultaneously occult references, inside jokes and brutally mocking jabs at the unaware (ie, most everybody).

TIME KEEPS ON SLIPPIN'...

In my first book, Chapter 26 is entitled, "The Illuminati End-of-Days Code," and in it I proposed that the precise time and date of the purported Mayan Apocalypse contained a code. December 21st is, of course, the winter solstice, and in 2012, the precise time of the solstice, I wrote, "as listed on the U.S. Naval Observatory's website *for years* in advance, was 11:11 Universal Time."

Thus, according to the faulty contemporary mythology, or urban legend, the exact moment of Galactic Alignment was 11:11 on 12/21/12. (We've been over the fact that Galactic Alignment has been occurring over the past 40 some odd years – and, in reality, the year in which the visual alignment was most precise was way back in 1998. More on that later.)

As I observed in the book, "New Agers and spiritualists went absolutely bonkers over this seeming super-synchronistic Message from the Matrix... *the Universe was speaking to us.* Entire books were written on the subject and there were more 11:11 YouTube videos than you could shake a stick at." Continuing,

> Nobody stopped to consider the alternative explanation: that, as opposed to being a loving message from the Creator indicating the impending ascension of mankind, this was yet another indicator of the exact depth of the tyranny humanity was now living under – a tyranny so pervasive that it extended into every aspect of our lives, of our existence, including *time* itself.
>
> Winter solstice: December 21st. 12/21. 11:11. If that looks strangely like a code to you, your instincts are correct... Do you not think that, being the insane control freaks they have repeatedly shown themselves to be, the Illuminati had some ingenious scheme for counting up (or counting down) to this most momentous of occasions...?
>
> 11:11 UT December 21st, 2012, was not simply a time and date. It was a *code*, one that reflected the very mathematical structure of the order of the ages:

11:11, 12/21
11 x 111 = 1221

Intriguing, you might be thinking, *but what does that really tell us?* For one thing, it hints at an ability to manipulate our reality that defies what most of us are willing to accept. But only *hints,* because that's not the full code…

Now, I'm going to spare you some of the other math I included in *9/11 as Mass Ritual* and get right to the numerical point:

1221 x 21 = 25641 = 777 x 33 = 77 x 333

I referred to 25641 as the Illuminati SuperNumber and as "a mathematical alchemical formulation capable of transmuting its very nature, much like the mythical phoenix. It is 777 and 33, the number of God and the number of Christ, and simultaneously 77 and 333, the number of Satan and the number of [the demon] Choronzon."

Even more pertinently, however, is that this number is very close to the *approximate* 26,000 years of the Great Age. While it is certainly true that any number of educated folk have speculated on the exact length of the Great Year, there is no widely-accepted answer – even if there was, how the hell would you know when to start the clock?

But we're not dealing with historical fact or objective truth here. It's all *make believe,* anyway. What matters is when the Cryptocracy *says* the Great Age begins, or, as importantly, ends.

FIDDLE DEE DEE

Twenty-one sets of 1221 also equals 231 sets of 111 – a calendrical system that tracks cycles of 1221, 111 … and 33.

What I was not aware of at the time I wrote about the end-of-days code in 2011 is that famed occultist Dr. John "the Original 007" Dee (1527-1608), Queen Elizabeth I's court advisor and astrologer (and the foremost scientific genius of the 16th century) at one time had proposed an official calendar based on sets of 33 years. Although this idea didn't originate with Dee, the calendar had certain advantages and theological-occult implications, but was officially rejected at the time. Was it, or some form of it, adopted by the Cryptocracy?

From an occult perspective, the attractiveness of a 33-based time-keeping system cannot be overstated. But consider this, as well. Here we have a system that tracks 21 sets of 1221 – with 12/21 corresponding to December 21st, the winter solstice, the day that the sun is at its lowest point in the sky, the annual symbolic "death" of the sun. (This is also the traditional date when the position of the sun against the backdrop of the Zodiac and Milky Way is measured and recorded for posterity – for the purposes of tracking its progress through the heavens and determining what time it is on the Precessional Clock.)

But 1221 what? Winter solstices? Years? If you track the winter solstices, it doesn't actually matter what the precise length of the year is, does it? Twenty-one sets of 1,221 winter solstices (12/21s)… the length of the Great Year, in Illuminati Time, which is the only time that truly matters.

MATHEMAGIC

We have then, or the Cryptocracy has, rather, a numerologically perfect time-keeping system to track the passage of the Cycle of Precession and to employ in reverse as a countdown to the End of the Age – which, if you'll recall, is coming up in 2021.

Hmmm… 1221 sets of 21. What would that look like as a date? December 21, 2021… 12/21/21.

KABOOM! But hold on, this won't *necessarily* be the date of the aforementioned hypothetical global nuclear false flag attack (although it'd sure seem like the opportune moment, but there's more to consider on this point). The real bombshell here is that on December 21st, 2021, *the date itself encodes the numbers of the cycle*, and the Number of Completion – *and that this officially marks the End of the Great Age.*

Not really.

The Number of the Beast

If you're a more or less normal person (whatever that means nowadays), you're probably sick and tired of the 111s by now – but I can't help it, we've got to go there again.

MAGIC SQUARE OF THE SUN

6	32	3	34	35	1	111
7	11	27	28	8	30	111
19	14	16	15	23	24	111
18	20	22	21	17	13	111
25	29	10	9	26	12	111
36	5	33	4	2	31	•111

111•111•111•111•111•111-666

Above is the ancient "Magic Square of the Sun," and I could explain it in detail, but you can look at the diagram and glean the important points: every row, and both diagonals, adds to 111, and the sum of the rows both vertically and horizontally is 666, which is thus closely associated with pagan sun worship (and is, of course, the number of the Beast in the Book of Revelation).

What has that got to do with our current discussion? Well, besides providing additional rationale for a 111-based calendar, there's this: 25 + 641 = 666.

HAPPY NEW YEAR

A FARAH KHAN FILM

CHAPTER THIRTEEN

IT'S ALL IN THE TIMING

As we start our little treasure hunt, we have a specific date to keep in mind, but *where* do we start looking? Where better than my favorite city and former workplace, the Occult Wonderland, Magickal Kingdom and Greatest Show on Earth, Washington, D.C.? There are a couple of things to keep in mind, though.

SERIOUS ABOUT SIRIUS

First, if December 21st, 2021 is The End of the *Current* Great Age, when does the *New* Great Age begin? December 22nd?! Not so fast. We're talking about the hypothetical end of an approximately 26,000-year cycle. This is not science. Again, it's whatever the Cryptocracy says it is.

A couple of days (or weeks, or months, or even years) here or there over the course of 26 millennia … pphht, who cares? Our rulers are insanely creative and they do not perform on cue. Whatever we think they might do, they almost certainly will not. They are infinitely smarter than us – who are we to think that we can figure out their incredibly well-laid and Satan-kissed plans in advance?

But, if I had to guess… I'd rule out December 22nd, 23rd and 24th, although the ancient Roman Saturnalia festival did run from December 17 to the 23rd. I'd also rule out Christmas Day as the official start of the New Great Age, although a massive nuclear false flag attack on this day would most certainly desecrate this highest of Christian holidays for all eternity. Even at that, it still seems a little too obvious.

(Left) Saturnalia.

I'd say maybe December 31st, 2021/January 1st, 2022, New Year's Eve/New Year's Day, and not because of some simple New Year = New Great Year formulation. No, the true appeal of New Year's lies in its connection to Sirius, the Blazing Star, seething with the energies of Lucifer.

AN EXERCISE IN FUTILITY

Most are unaware that our New Year begins when Sirius reaches its zenith in mid-heaven at mid-night. And I believe that it is much more likely that the Cryptocracy would greet the first zenith attainment of Sirius in the New Great Age and use this as its Official Welcome, rather than greeting the first rising of the reborn sun on Christmas Day in the dawning Great Year. Our masters do not worship the sun. They worship Sirius.

The Dawn of the New Great Age: January 1st, 2022 (1/1/22…1122… that looks kinda familiar…). Note that we could well find cryptic/hidden references to both 2021, as the End of the Passing Great Year, and 2022, as the Dawn of the New Great Age (of Satan).

Also note that there may be no attacks on NYE-NYD 2021-2022. Even if I'm entirely correct about the significance of these dates to the Cryptocracy, that doesn't automatically mean that they'll stage a false flag then. Attempting to predict their intentions or actions with any degree of accuracy is a futile exercise, a fact that I've learned repeatedly over the years.

A TURN OF THE WHEEL

The second thing to keep in mind is this: there are many examples, spanning eons and diverse civilizations, of time being expressed, or encoded, as distance. In fact, several instances of this practice can be found in the Bible.

Similarly, as we will see, a specific geographic location can be considered to represent not just the physical center of heaven, the City of God, but also the *center of time*. The Alpha and the Omega. The beginning and the end. The completion of one cycle concurrent with the initiation of the next. One full revolution of the wheel. One full circuitous journey through the signs of the Zodiac.

COSMIC CAPITOL

The Potomac River: the Milky Way Galaxy. Capitol Hill: the Cosmic Mountain, Galactic Center (not the *exact* center, but the "nuclear bulge"). The Capitol Dome: the Womb of Isis, also a symbol of Galactic Center. Classic precessional geography, symbology and architecture.

Washington, DC: the center of the heavens, Heaven (as incongruous as this may sound in today's political climate), the City of God. Like the ancient Mayan temples, the city of Washington, DC, was aligned to the stars and encodes a galactic cosmology.

This Celestial City was designed in the ancient tradition. Like Stonehenge and innumerable sites and cities since, it is aligned with the summer and winter solstices, and DC's streets and architecture encode various other astronomical features and alignments. But the most powerful city in the world is more than a giant astronomical observatory or the heavens set in stone. It is, far more significantly, a giant time piece, an enormous Precessional Clock. (Don't think I can prove it? Clue: What do you wind a clock with, and which monument sits almost dead center on the National Mall?)

The New Jerusalem

Christian conservatives contend that America was founded on Judeo-Christian principles. Whether or not you believe this to be true, its capital city was most certainly not built to honor the LORD/Jehovah/YHWH/Yahwey.

Ironically, the sacrilegious elite did establish the boundaries of the city, which is laid out as a square, in what might be viewed as a scale 2-D version of the New Jerusalem, the Biblical "City of God," whose dimensions are described in the Book of Revelation. (There's more on this later.)

Remember, *everything* is dark humor, mockery, irreverent inversion and sacrilege – the blasphemous mindset of the Black Mass applied to anything you can think of.

CHAPTER FOURTEEN

Birthday Bash

The year 1976, the bicentennial of the United States of America, and the country held a fitting year-long 200th birthday party.

(Far right) *Adam Weishaupt, founder of the Illuminati*

The year of the nation's founding, 1776, was also the year of the establishment of the Illuminati, and thus 1976 marked a second important bicentennial. In addition, the very special year of 1776 marked an altogether different occasion.

Countdown Initiated

Recall that Dr. John Dee's Illuminati Precessional Calendar facilitates the tracking of blocks of 111 years. Counting up, that's 21 x 11 x 111 = 25641. Counting *down*, on the other hand, by sets of 111 to the end of the Great Age as marked by the year of most-precise Galactic Alignment, 1998, the final set of 111 would begin in 1887. Ah ha! But what does that mean?

The year 1887 saw the first Groundhog Day observed in Punxsutawney, Pennsylvania, and the first *Glenfiddich* single-malt Scotch whisky produced. Much more significantly, it was also the year of the founding of the Hermetic Order of the Golden Dawn, of which famed occultist Aleister Crowley was a member.

However, this last item could have merely been coincidence (although anyone familiar with Crowley would have to wonder), and thus the year 1887 might well signify absolutely nothing. No, what we want to do is back up another 111 years, which puts us at, yes, 1776 – which would mean that the founding of America was timed to coincide with the initiation of the last two cycles of 111 on the long countdown to the End of All Things. Seventeen seventy six: 222 years to Galactic Alignment, and counting.

COUNTING DOWN, AGAIN

Yes, but… 1998 was not the end of all things, of course, and nothing even happened that year that could have been part of a celebration or commemoration by the Cryptocracy to mark the occasion… right? I'm fairly certain (positive, actually) that you'll want to withhold judgment on that last point until later on, but remember this: we aren't necessarily looking for a single countdown to a single date or year.

We are talking about the end of the Great Age, a once-in-a-26,000-year occasion. The elite may well have established multiple countdowns, marking the opening of the Galactic Alignment window (which, by the way, was 1976),[1] the "precise" moment of Galactic Alignment itself in 1998, and the closing of the window in 2021-2022.

---

1. Some say 1974, but I'll once again repeat that the only opinion that matters on this or any other point is that of the psychopaths who rule the planet, and having the celebrations surrounding the country's bicentennial in 1976 double as an in-plain-sight "Opening of the Galactic Alignment Window" ritual makes absolutely perfect sense.

Seriously? No, I'm just making stuff up. You can ignore the fact that both the White House and the U.S. Capitol Building both went into service in the year 1800 – the former on November 1 (11/1...that's 111 for the numerologically impaired) and the latter on November 17. And while you're at it, completely forget that 1800 plus 222 equals 2022.

The Galactic Alignment Birthday Boy

In *9/11 as Mass Ritual*, I wrote about Ted Olson, U.S. Solicitor under President George W. Bush from June 2001 to July 2004, referring to him as the "9/11 birthday boy":

> As fate would have it, Mr. Olson was born on September 11, 1940, and, as fate would also have it, Olson's third wife, Barbara, just happened to be a passenger on hijacked American Airlines Flight 77 – which, on September 11, 2001, crashed into the Pentagon, for which the groundbreaking ceremony was held on September 11, 1941.

(Left) *Cropping of the* Scene at the Signing of the Constitution of the United States *by Howard Chandler Christy, 1940. Washington, presiding officer, stands at right. (Right)* Washington as Farmer at Mount Vernon *by Junius Brutus Stearns, 1851.*

George Washington, before he became known much more recently through insanely-liberal revisionist history as primarily a slave-owning honky possessed of copious quantities of white privilege, was formerly widely recognized as one of the Founding Fathers of the United States and as the nation's first President.

Washington's critical role in leading Patriot forces to victory over the British and their allies during the American Revolutionary War, his presiding at the Constitutional Convention of 1787, and his two terms as President led to him being referred to as the "Father of His Country."

Washington was also a Master Mason and shortly before becoming our first president was elected the first Worshipful Master of Alexandria Lodge No. 22. In taking the presidential oath of office, Washington used the Bible of the St. John's Masonic Lodge No. 1 of New York, and prominent Mason and Chancellor of New York Robert Livingston administered the oath.

A little known fact about our first president is that he was very self-conscious about his hands. No, not really. If you've never heard of the "hidden hand," you should read up on it.

As recorded by his personal secretary, "'Tis well" were Washington's last words when he died in 1799, and one supposes that all was well for him until 1830 when a disgruntled ex-employee of the Mount Vernon estate attempted to steal his skull – which, as we know, is a symbol of Galactic Center.

And that reminds me of the point of all this, which is that Washington was born in 1732 on February 22nd – 2/22. George "222" Washington, Galactic Alignment Birthday Boy. It sure pays to be born on the right day.

CHAPTER FIFTEEN

LOCATION, LOCATION, LOCATION

BONUS QUESTION: *The Potomac River represents the Milky Way galaxy, and the U.S. Capitol represents Galactic Center (ie. the Cosmic Mountain). Where in the landscape/layout of Washington, D.C., could we expect to find Galactic Alignment itself encoded?*

Remember, the grand alignment doesn't take place at the precise center of the Milky Way's nuclear bulge, but about 6 degrees to one side along the Galactic Equator (GE) where it is intersected by the plane of the ecliptic (sun's path through the sky, PE), which forms the Great Cross. (Note that this is not necessarily a vertical, perpendicular cross: the GE and PE do not meet at a right angle.)

Where to look for a symbolic representation of the Great Cross? Well, obviously there are more intersecting streets in DC than you can shake a stick at. Let's narrow it down a bit, and look for a major thoroughfare representing the Galactic Equator, originating at or passing through the U.S. Capitol (Galactic Center) and intersected by a street representing the plane of the ecliptic.

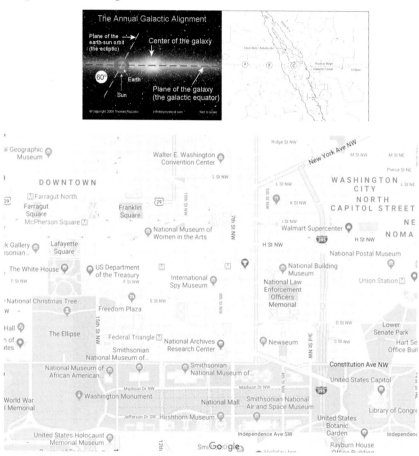

Maryland Avenue Southwest originates directly in front of the Capitol, and is intersected by exactly zero major thoroughfares before terminating near the Tidal Basin (okay, technically it ends in a roundabout). Pennsylvania Avenue Northwest likewise originates at the Capitol and runs almost directly into the White House grounds. If extended to the White House itself, it would be intersected there by New York Avenue Northwest if it, too, were extended a short distance to the White House.

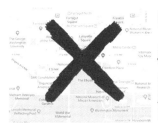

Bingo. X marks the spot. More precisely, the White House marks "The Place of Crossing," with New York Avenue serving as the plane of the ecliptic and Pennsylvania Avenue as the Galactic Equator.

Now, if your first reaction to this proposition is, *That's ridiculous*, I understand. But I'm not finished making my case yet, not by a long shot.

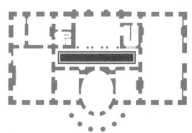

(Left) A diagram showing the location of the main hall on the first floor of the White House. (Right) A photo of the hall, which, interestingly enough in context of the current discussion, is named "Cross Hall." (The White House, dead center of the terrestrial representation of the Great Cross, and Cross Hall, dead center of the White House.)

An Open Window

So, I'm suggesting that the White House sits at the precise center of a terrestrial representation of the Great Celestial Cross, and that a conceptual miniature sun has slowly travelled up New York Avenue NW, aka the plane of the ecliptic, to arrive there in our era? Yes, more or less. And by extension, I am proposing that the White House and its immediate grounds represent the 40-year *window* of Galactic Alignment. Laughable?

Fine. If in our hypothetical concrete-and-steel DC Precessional Clock our happy little sun has dawdled up New York Ave towards the White House, where it has almost finished crossing our imaginary Galactic Equator, then all of this would be symbolized in some fashion, wouldn't it?

As a matter of fact, it is, but I'll warn you – if you get too literal with all this, you're gonna be frustrated and disappointed. (I *knoooow* that there's only a small section of NY Ave to the west of the White House.) I'm not asking you to suspend your rational faculties, I'm telling you not to be anal-retentive. All of this, you have to keep in mind, is a damn joke on some profound level.

There's an owl, the Owl of Moloch (or Minerva, I don't care), designed into the grounds around the U.S. Capitol, for God's sake ... and much more of this silliness on the National Mall, but that's fun for later.

ZIP-A-DEE DOO-DAH

The center of the Great Cross – symbolized on our Precessional Clock by the White House – is synchronous with the precise year of Galactic Alignment, 1998, and the White House grounds correspond to a 40-year window that closes at the end of 2021.

Our sun has travelled northwest up NY Ave, has already moved largely off of the Great White House Cross and is about to clear the imaginary Galactic Equator (represented by the non-existent section of Pennsylvania Avenue running diagonally through the White House). It will be completely beyond the equator of the Milky Way by the close of 2021, and thus by the beginning of 2022 the alignment will be officially over and the New Great Age will be set to start.

So, if I'm correct about all this, what do you think that the zip code of the block immediately to the east of the White House – 1500 Pennsylvania Ave NW, home to the U.S. Department of the Treasury, towards which the rapidly setting imaginary sun of our current Great Year is headed – would be? 20220. Zip-a-dee Doo-Dah. Thank you very much.

THE CORRECT ADDRESS

Still not convinced? Tough crowd. Again, the White House and its immediate environs on one level encode the end of the current Great Age. The length of that age, as we know from previous discussion, is, on the only clock that matters, 25,641.

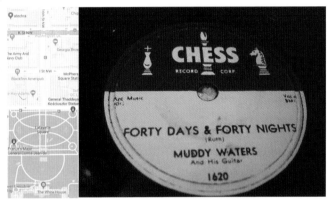

The White House is located at 1600 Pennsylvania Avenue. If 16th Street NW didn't dead-end into Lafayette Square, which sits to the immediate north of the White House, it would run directly through it. Multiplying 1600 by 16 yields 25,600, a mere 41 units short of the length of the Illuminati Great Year. Coincidence?

The entire 1600 *block* of Pennsylvania Avenue represents the *window* of Galactic Alignment, which spans 40 years, give or take a little: 25,600 + 41 = 25,641. Pretty simple, and pretty plain, don't you think? (If you wanna haggle over plus-or-minus one year across the span of almost 26 centuries, be my guest. But keep this in mind: 25,641 can also be expressed as $4^2 \times 40^2 + 40 + 1$ ...very Biblical.)

A BIG ZERO

The physical address of the White House encoding the number of completion, the full number of the Illuminati Great Age, 25641: that's quite a notion, as is the idea of the White House itself sitting at dead center of a terrestrial representation of the Celestial Great Cross, symbolizing Galactic Alignment, and, thus the transition from one Great Age to the next.

But is not the Omega one with the Alpha, the end of the old cycle simultaneously the beginning of the new? Is this not the Zero Point? It is, and, similarly, as we count up, we also count down, to zero. *And lo and behold*, what do we find directly across the street from the South Lawn of the White House but the Zero Milestone.

The winged helmet of Mercury, god of travel, is found on the Zero Milestone. The Roman Mercury, Greek Hermes and Egyptian Thoth are all held to be manifestations of the same deity, with Thoth being "the reckoner of times and seasons," a god of the measurement and regulation of events and of time itself.

Originally envisioned as the American equivalent to Rome's Golden Milestone, or *Milliarium Aureum*, from which all roads were considered to begin and all distances in the Roman Empire measured, the Zero Milestone never realized its stated purpose, and currently only roads in the Washington, D.C., area are measured from it.

Perhaps, though, it has been fulfilling its *true* purpose all along. The engraving on the side of the monument facing south towards the Washington Monument reads:

POINT FOR THE
MEASUREMENT
OF DISTANCES
FROM WASHING-
TON ON HIGH
WAYS OF THE
UNITED STATES

Note that the word "Washington" is hyphenated, whereas the word "highways" is not, and thus it reads, "high ways" – as in "the *high ways* of magic."

House of the Rising Sun?

Speaking of magic… Just to make sure we all have this straight, the White House is basically the "House of the Rising Sun," ie., the rising sun of the New Great Age. Yet, if this were indeed true, wouldn't it be signified in a more direct, more tangible manner? Good point. Yes, it probably would.

Return to the aforementioned Lafayette Square, which, before it became a public park, was used as a racetrack, a graveyard, a zoo and a slave market. The square was designed by Andrew Jackson Downing (pictured above right), considered to be a founder of American landscape architecture. Look closely at its design from an aerial perspective. It rather resembles some magic symbol, don't you think? A planetary seal, perhaps?

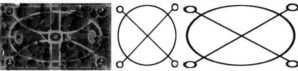

(Left) Lafayette Square. (Center) The Planetary Seal of Jupiter. (Right) Elongated version.

The Planetary Seal of Jupiter (above)? *Possibly, but that's kinda weak…*

(Left) The Planetary Seal of the Sun. (Center) Elongated version. (Right) Lafayette Square.

The ancient Planetary Seal of the Sun? (Yes, I realize the sun is not a planet – I didn't invent this term.) I don't know, perhaps the park design is a simplified version of the seal…

Or, maybe the design is simply what popped into Downing's head when he sat down to draw up a plan. Consider this, however. The White House and grounds are The Place of Crossing, where the sun and earth align at the Great Cross. What would it look like if we combined the astrological earth symbol and the Seal of the Sun?

(Left) Earth symbol. (Center) Elongated. (Right) Combined.

Pretty darn close. (Okay, you tell me how *you* would better translate the combined symbols into the design for a public park. If you can do it, I'll kiss your foot.) These two joined elements form a gargantuan magic sigil in the landscape, esoterically branding this location as the The Place of Crossing, which we already know it to be. How's that for tangible?

THE WICKER MAN

CHRISTOPHER LEE
BRITT EKLAND
DIANE CILENTO
EDWARD
WOODWARD
INGRID PITT

LE DIEU D'OSIER

SCENARIO
ANTHONY SHAFFER
(FRENZY & SLEUTH)

COLOR

PROD. PETER SNELL
REGIE: ROBIN HARDY

DE GEVLOCHTEN GOD

CHAPTER SIXTEEN

THE RITE STUFF

W hile the nation was occupied with its 200th birthday celebration during 1976, there was a party of a different sort taking place in New York City, one that achieved worldwide notoriety.

XTRA SPECIAL

S ince part of this was tucked into a footnote in Chapter 14, I'll repeat it:

> …the opening of the Galactic Alignment window…was 1976…the celebrations surrounding the country's bicentennial in 1976 double as an in-plain-sight "Opening of the Galactic Alignment Window" ritual.

Given all we know at this point, that would certainly makes sense, but what form did the ritual take?

Let's play a little game.

Closely examine this image (far left):

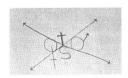

The central "X" forms the framework for the assemblage – note the directional arrows on the ends of the two line segments indicating that they extend in each direction. (This is how one would represent, just for example, the intersection between the plane of the ecliptic and the Galactic Equator.)

You'll note the planetary symbols for Venus to the immediate left of the center of the X and Mars to the right – and since we all know which planet orbits the sun between Venus and Mars, this would seem to indicate that we are to infer that the Earth is sitting dead center of the X. But we don't have to infer it.

We know from the last chapter/sidebar that the planetary symbol for Earth is a cross within a circle, but this symbol is not present. However, that is only one of the symbols used to represent our planet. Another is a stylized *globus cruciger* (Latin for "cross-bearing orb"), but that's obviously not present, either.

Long before its adoption by Christianity as its primary symbol, the cross – which we see in the image sitting directly above, and anchored in, the Xs center point – was used by a wide range of spiritual traditions to represent a variety of things, including, unsurprisingly, the Earth. The four arms of the cross can be seen to represent the four cardinal directions, and also the cross formed by Earth's equator and axis.

For alchemists, the cross was a symbol of air, earth, fire and water, the four "classical elements." It has also been used to symbolize the union of heaven and earth, human and divine.

ONE GUESS

Recapping what we've established thus far, we have the Earth sitting atop the center of a big fat X. Proceeding, we observe that underneath the cross is the letter S. Anyone care to venture a guess as to what that might stand for?

Okay, I'm not going to further belabor the point here. I'm obviously insinuating that the image is an encoding of Galactic Alignment. But so what?

So what, is that it was taken from one of the letters allegedly written by the Son of Sam killer, David Richard Berkowitz, whose killing spree started in the summer of 1976, the year of the opening of the Galactic Alignment window.

A MATTER OF INTERPRETATION

Feel free to challenge my interpretation of these elements. After all, the planetary sign for Venus is also the female gender symbol, just as the sign for Mars is the male gender symbol. And perhaps if the cross *does* represent Christ/Christianity here, the "S" represents Satan/Satanism. The lower half of the Venus sign is oddly elongated, suggesting an inverted cross, a key symbol in Satan worship.

Before you dismiss my interpretation, however, you should also be aware that on December 21ˢᵗ, 2012, the Observed Year of Galactic Alignment and the date of the Mayan Non-Apocalypse, Venus and Mars were directly on either side of the Great Galactic Cross on the plane of the ecliptic.

So, we're gonna go with my interpretation, which I admit might be inaccurate in some fashion, but if you're really worked up about it, go write your own book.

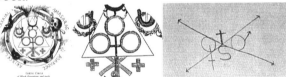

Some researchers assert that Berkowitz's symbol was derived from the Goetic Circle of Black Evocations *(specifically, the circled portion in the image) by French occult author and ceremonial magician Éliphas Lévi. I'm still gonna go with my interpretation.*

LOOKING DEEPER

Now, before we get stuck on an obvious question like, *Why would a deranged serial killer supposedly incorporate a drawing encoding Galactic Alignment into one of his letters?*, we need to back up and question a key assumption underlying it.

Namely, was Berkowitz *solely* responsible for all of the killings attributed to him (even those that he confessed to and had detailed knowledge of)? Many books have been written on this case, including quite a few that challenge the official "lone gunman" storyline, and there are some compelling indications that Berkowitz had accomplices.

Beyond this, there are indications not simply that there were other people involved, but that there were dark ritualistic dimensions to the slayings. In fact, during the mid-1990s, Berkowitz amended his confession, claiming that he had been a member of a violent Satanic cult that orchestrated the killings as ritual murders.

Even if this were true, however, that doesn't mean that we've gotten to the bottom of the matter or discovered its true nature – or identified its ultimate orchestrators.

A GALACTIC RIDDLE

As previously mentioned, one of the general symbols for Galactic Center is a womb, and, more specifically, the Womb of Isis. Horus is the son of Isis (and Osiris, sort of…it's kinda hard to sire offspring without a penis), and he most often depicted as a falcon or as a man with a falcon head – even his hieroglyph was a falcon.

(Left) God Horus as a falcon wearing the Double Crown of Egypt. 27th dynasty. State Museum of Egyptian Art, Munich

According to arch occultist and Godfather of Modern Satanism, Aleister Crowley, the sacred number of Horus is 44, and we currently are living in the Aeon of Horus. (In Crowley's *Liber 44: Mass of the Phoenix*, a bell is rung a total of 44 times during the ritual.)

Let's continue our game with a few fill-in-the-blanks:

Fill in
the blank:
____

Fill in the blank #1:
Berkowitz's birth name was Richard David _____.

Fill in the blank #2:
Berkowitz used a ____ caliber Bulldog revolver and was also known as the "____ Caliber Killer."

Fill in the blank #3:
Berkowitz drove a Ford _____.

Of course I'm not going to make you go look up the answers if you don't already know them (and why would you?). They are: Falco,[1] 44 and Galaxie.

Falcon, 44 and Galaxy. If you want to accuse me of cherry picking details to support my pet theory, that's your right, but before you do, you should thoroughly familiarize yourself with the *numerous* synchronistic elements of the case (which you can chalk up to mere coincidence if you're so inclined, or to conspiracy, or Satan, I don't care). I'm not going to attempt to list them all here, but I'll go over some of the more pertinent ones.

A BEHEMOTH

In his letters to police, Berkowitz referenced "The Twenty Two Disciples of Hell," and, in 1976, twenty two years remained until the most precise moment of Galactic Alignment in 1998.

Okay, that one *could* be coincidence (although I'd wait until reading the endnote at the end of this chapter before making a decision on this), but he also referenced "Wicked King Wicker," prompting police to arrange a private screening of the 1973 horror movie starring Christopher Lee entitled, *The Wicker Man* – the plot of which, as most of you probably know, revolves around ritual sacrificial murder.

(Right) Conjuring echoes of Sirhan Sirhan, Charles Manson (probably) and other numerous subjects of MK-Ultra, Manchurian-Candidate-style mind-control programs, in one of Berkowitz's letters he makes the statement that he was "programmed too [sic] kill."

Also worth noting is that, as explained by Michael Hoffman in *Secret Societies and Psychological Warfare*, Éliphas Lévi, born Alphonse Louis Constant, chose his first name "as a play on the Latin word for elephant, *elephas*, whose demon familiar is supposed to be the 'Behemoth.'"

(Left) The world-famous rendering of Baphomet, from Éliphas Lévi's Dogme et Rituel de la Haute Magie, 1856. (Center) The Elephus disco. (Right) Behemoth, the demon of gluttony, as portrayed by the occultist-journalist Collin de Plancy in the 1863 edition of his Dictionnaire Infernal. Behemoth was the infernal watchman, presiding over gluttonous banquets and feasts, and was considered Hell's official singer.

71

In a letter found at the site of one of the Son of Sam murders, the killer had written, "I am the 'monster' – 'Beelzebub' – the 'Chubby Behemoth,'" and subsequently, another of the murders was committed at the Elephas disco in the Bayside section of Queens.

Speaking of Behemoths, I probably don't need to elaborate on this, but, as I wrote on page 124 of 9/11 as Mass Ritual, "In 2000, the year in which Bonesman G.W. Bush was elected, the Republican logo was changed from its original configuration, left, to the one shown on the right – with three inverted pentagrams – which is still in use."

Dog Days

Satire is quite important in the occult scheme, especially as epilogue. Mockery is the ne plus ultra of ceremonial murder.
  – Michael Hoffman, Secret Societies and Psychological Warfare

David Berkowitz initially claimed that he was taking orders from a demon-possessed black Labrador retriever named Sam (the dog was actually named Harvey), and, further, that he'd attempted to kill the dog but was thwarted by supernatural means. (Some people, and I couldn't argue with them, would contend that *all* Labrador retrievers are possessed.)

Now I realize we're talking about serial murder, but that's funny. I mean, just because the guy allegedly killed a bunch of people doesn't mean he doesn't have a sense of humor.

(Left) A talking animal named Harvey, eh? (Center) Sirius the Police Dog. (Right) The 17th tarot, The Star.

In *9/11 as Mass Ritual*, I explained how another Labrador retriever served as a living (and then dead) symbol of Sirius:

> We've met Sirius, the Dog Star, the shining light of the occultists, whose pernicious presence is ubiquitous throughout the 9/11 MegaRitual. Now, meet Sirius, the Police Dog, the only such animal to be killed in the attack on the Twin Towers, who died in his kennel in the basement of Tower Two when it collapsed.
>
> Sirius, a four-and-a-half-year-old ninety pound yellow Labrador Retriever, was an Explosive Detection Dog with the Port Authority of New York and New Jersey Police Department. It just so happens that Sirius' badge number was 17, and the 17th card in the Tarot is…wait for it…The Star, which, according to many occultists, depicts (what else?) – Sirius.

Was the demon dog story a crafty strategy to embed the Sirius meme into the Son of Sam Mass Ritual? I'd bet so (although there's actually much more going on than meme-making, I'll elaborate on that soon) – and then there's this: in December 1976, Berkowitz killed a dog named Rocket (hey, not bad if you're going for broke with the whole Inter-Galactic Freak Show thing, Jack Parsons would be proud) at 18 Wicker Street. Two days later, three German shepherds were found in a gutter adjacent to…Wicker Street.

WORD PLAY

Who would, who *could*, orchestrate a grisly mass-terror ritual of this scope and character? Berkowitz stated that, "There are other Sons out there, God help the world" – other Sons of Sam. But did he mean other members of a Satanic cult, or…?

(Left) Samson Destroying the Temple of the Philistines, by Giovanni Benedetto Castiglione (17 C.). (Right) Eat your heart out, Delilah.

Perhaps in all the clues purposefully left behind we can find a cryptic claim of responsibility that will save us the trouble of guessing. Sons of Sam – there are those who will tell you that, in times past, members of a very famous secretive fraternal organization were once known as "Sam's Sons."

In this centuries-old world-wide group, the Biblical Samson, who held up the two pillars of the Temple of Dagon, was used as an allegorical

73

archetype in their teachings. Thus, "Sam's Sons," which, if you'll note, is also a play on words (you know, sorta like Éliphas-*elephas*).

The name of this organization? The Freemasons.[2]

Endnotes

1. Surely I am not suggesting that Berkowitz was somehow chosen for his role, in part or in large, because of his birth name… hell, ask Berkowitz himself, who stated in a letter withheld from scrutiny for four years by police, "I David Berkowitz have been chosen since birth, to be one of the executioners of the cult." So there.

2. Certainly not any appreciable percentage of Freemasons would be involved in such nefarious activities – only a very few in the upper echelons, at most. Also, I am aware that it has been proposed that "Sam" is short for Samhain, and I guess one might also consider Samael, but in my opinion, any Satanic organizations or other cults that might've been involved, such as the OTO or Process Church of the Final Judgment, are at least one rung down on the ladder.

Not to be overlooked in all this is that, in the early fifth century, Latin philosopher Macrobius, whose most important work is the *Saturnalia*, noted in his *Chronicon* that the annual ancient Egyptian celebration of Horus was held on the winter solstice, a fact backed up by Epiphanius of Salamis in his most significant work, the *Panarion*. Winter solstice, December 21st, 12/21…1221…our Fiddle Dee Dee Precessional Clock is set to *"Horus Time"*!

Also, as mentioned earlier in this chapter, "In his letters to police, Berkowitz referenced 'The Twenty Two Disciples of Hell', and, in 1976, twenty two years remained until the most precise moment of Galactic Alignment in 1998." Adding 22 to 1998, we arrive at 2020, the last full year of the current Great Age (2021 is the Year of Transition, since, technically, the End of the Great Age is 12/21/21 – in Horus Time).

Thus, 1976 not only marked a 22-year countdown to Galactic Alignment Proper, but also a 44-year countdown to the Last Full Year of the Current Great Age. The Final Forty-Four.

Horus! Crowley! We're gonna party like it's 1998!

CHAPTER SEVENTEEN

STAR-CROSSED

A t this point, you probably don't want to hear anything else about
crosses, but we have to discuss this. Referencing the images below, as the earth's and sun's orientation to the Galactic Equator
(GE) change during the Cycle of Precession, the angles formed by the
earth's equinoctial and solstitial axes in relation to GE vary substantially.

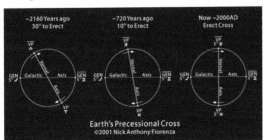

As we and our star approach Galactic Alignment, the solstitial axis becomes increasingly parallel to GE and the equinoctial axis increasingly perpendicular, and during the alignment, a cross is formed by the latter axis and the GE. It is variously referred to as the Precessional Cross and the Erect Cross.

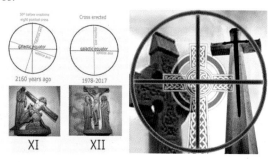

https://www.lunarplanner.com/HolyCross.html
http://www.treeincarnation.com/solar-phoenix-rebirth_part2.htm

You can see that in its symbolic form, the Erect Cross is essentially identical to (see images below) the planetary symbol for Earth, which of course we're already familiar with … or, a set of rifle-scope crosshairs … or, a Celtic cross … or, even this last image, which might simply look like a hand-drawn Celtic cross, but, as you're most likely aware, is in fact something altogether more sinister.

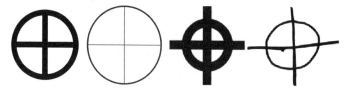

It is, of course, the symbol used by the Zodiac Killer (whose work pre-dated the Son of Sam murders by about 10 years) as his signature. Investigators concluded that the Zodiac killer had adopted the symbol because it was the logo used by the watchmaker of the same name – certainly a logical conclusion.

(Right) "Zodiac Watch Company, 44th Street, New York City" – Horus Time!

The killer's adoption of a watch company's logo could also be a way of communicating the following message: This is all about *TIME*.

A Means to An End

The Zodiac. The Precessional Cross. A time piece. How better to implant the most relevant memes and symbols into the mass consciousness in the run up to Galactic Alignment than through a series of terrifying unsolved murders?

(Left) The Clint Eastwood classic Dirty Harry *drew upon the Zodiac Killer case and featured this classic line: "... being this is a .44 Magnum, the most powerful handgun in the world and would blow your head clean off, you've gotta ask yourself one question: 'Do I feel lucky?' Well, do ya, punk?" (Far right) The case even inspired a 1971 porn flick featuring the legendary John Holmes.*

The case of the Zodiac Killer – which remains unsolved, only adding to its continuing valence – has over the past half century had such a powerful and lasting influence on the American psyche that it would be difficult to quantify its impact. It has inspired hundreds of books, movies and television programs, even influencing popular music.

(Left) During the 2016 U.S. Presidential campaign, a "Ted Cruz is the Zodiac Killer" meme went viral on the internet, with the primary problem being not that the mock conspiracy theory was totally implausible, but rather that it wasn't in the least funny. (Right) Now that's funny.

However, as alluded to in the last chapter when considering whether the demon dog story was just "a crafty strategy to embed the Sirius meme into the Son of Sam Mass Ritual," here, too, there's much more going on than meme-making, and much more at stake. Implanting "the most relevant memes and symbols" is not a goal unto itself, but rather a means to an end.

RITUAL MURDER AS MIND CONTROL

Michael Hoffman is a former reporter for the New York bureau of the Associated Press, and is the author of the seminal *Secret Societies and Psychological Warfare*, the first edition of which was published in 1989. I quote Hoffman liberally in both my books.

In *Secret Societies*, Hoffman observes that "ritual murder is mind control," and refers to the machinery of manipulation as "a technological tyranny so immense it is difficult to grasp. It is both a physical, technological tyranny as well as a tyranny of the mind," and involves "psycho-spiritual warfare methods hyped by 'coincidence,' symbolism and ritual."

Hoffman explains that it is the subconscious mind that is being targeted in occult ritual. "In occult crimes the objective is not linear," he states, "that is to say, is not solely bound to the achievement of the immediate effects of the attack on the victim, but may in fact be a part of a larger, symbolic ritual magnified by the power of the electronic media, for the purpose of the alchemical processing of the subconscious Group Mind of the masses." Hoffman continues, telling us that "it is the subconscious that is being addressed in occult ritual, in a process CIA behavioral scientist Dr. Ewan Cameron termed, 'psychic driving.'"

"The induction of terror into the mass mind of Americans in association with certain key-words and key-symbols or 'sigils' in connection with control-symbols," Hoffman states, "is the most efficacious means of ensuring a brain-dead and mind-controlled, subject population." He continues, asserting that "symbolism embedded within terrorism and achieved with seeming invincible accomplishment by 'invisible' principals, is a great way to control and process people."

Certain cases involving alleged serial killers, Hoffman contends, with good reason, "are ritual murders involving a cult protected by the U.S. government and the corporate media, with strong ties to the police."

Such killings are actually intricately choreographed ceremonies; performed first on a very intimate and secret scale, among the initiates themselves in order to program them, then on a grand scale, amplified incalculably by the electronic media.

In the end, what we have is a highly symbolic, ritual working broadcast to millions of people, a Satanic inversion; a Black Mass, where the "pews" are filled by the entire nation and through which humanity is brutalized and debased in this, the "Nigredo" phase of the alchemical process.

"The Black Arts adepts who wear police badges, occupy judge's seats and media editor's desks," he concludes, "are not simply 'crazed', nor are such intensely publicized ritual murders merely superstitious sacrifices to some kooky devil-god." They are in fact "a brilliantly orchestrated ritual whose ceremonial aspects were as precise and detailed as the internal workings of a clock," and constitute an "alchemical psychodrama for the processing of humanity."

Hoffman also addresses the difficulty we have accepting the idea that we could be manipulated unbeknownst and on a mass scale:

> The issue of controlling humanity with esoteric words and symbols encoded within a play, a media spectacular or a ritual is one of the most difficult for people to comprehend. ...Even as [modern man] dances to the tune of the elite managers of human behavior, he scoffs with great derision at the idea of the existence and operation of a technology of mass mind control emanating from the media and government.

We do not believe, therefore we do not see.

Sam I Am?

Was, then, the Zodiac Killer's signature symbol also an encoding of Galactic Alignment? You know what I think. And just maybe there's an even deeper connection between the Son of Sam killings and the Zodiac Killer.

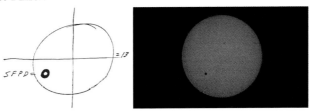

(Left) A variation on the Zodiac Killer's signature symbol from one of his letters. (Right) A photograph of a planet in front of the sun.

In October, 1969, someone claiming to be the Zodiac called the Oakland Police Department, demanding that one of two prominent lawyers appear on a local television show. This was arranged, and the host appealed to the viewers to keep the lines open. Eventually, someone claiming to be the Zodiac called several times, claiming his name was... "Sam."[1]

---

1. I actually have no idea whether any of the same perpetrators were involved in both cases, but I can tell you that the number of instances in which I've found one false flag attack or mass ritual clearly foreshadowed or pre-figured in some fashion in an earlier event of a similar nature are too numerous to count. And even if this is just coincidence in this particular case, I don't care, because I think this is a cool way to end the chapter.

CHAPTER EIGHTEEN

DIRTY TALK

Returning now to the Magick Year, 1998, and the Magickal King-dom, Washington, D.C., there I was, still working at the *Weekly Standard* magazine, one of then-President Bill Clinton's harshest critics.

As I began my third year as art director of the neo-conservative week-ly political magazine, I had no idea what the first few weeks of January were to bring.

Led by William Kristol, former Vice-President Dan Quayle's chief-of-staff, the magazine, although less well known outside the Beltway than *National Review*, had significant influence in the halls of Washington, with its writers and editors becoming a ubiquitous presence in the local and national media.

A LITTLE TO THE LEFT

For the two years since the publication's inception in 1995, weekly staff meetings had generally been a fairly low-key routine, with live-ly-but-civil discussions regarding domestic and foreign policy, sociocultural matters and the like, rarely progressing beyond any subject that would require more than a PG rating. Beginning in the third week of January, 1998, however, this would change to a degree that I wouldn't have imagined possible just several weeks earlier.

NEWSWEEK KILLS STORY ON WHITE HOUSE INTERN; BLOCKBUSTER REPORT: 23-YEAR OLD, SEX RELATIONSHIP WITH PRESIDENT

DRUDGE REPORT

On January 17th, news of the Monica Lewinsky scandal first broke on the *Drudge Report*, and our staff meetings would soon of necessity include the tawdry details of the affair, including semen-stained blue dresses, which direction the Commander-in-Chief's member lists (to port, if I recall correctly), and which objects he did or did not insert in his former intern's vagina (cigar, yes; penis, no).

(Right) Fast forward 20 years from '98 to 2018 and not much has improved since the Lewinsky scandal – porn actress Stormy Daniels publically claimed that President Donald Trump's johnson is shaped like a 'shroom.

I designed, or commissioned artwork for, quite a few Clinton-scandal related magazine covers.

Cheap Thrills

As the Year of the Grand Alignment commenced, and the sun hung upon the Great Celestial Cross, the air was thick/laden/potent with meaning and mystery (or, it could have been the fumes from heavy Beltway traffic).

Yet, there was to be no massive false-flag-attack-cum-mass-ritual as there soon would be in 2001. No human sacrifice, no death and destruction – not even any good memes. What the hell kind of way was this to commemorate Galactic Alignment Proper?

In Washington, D.C. – the Most Powerful City in the World, whose streets, buildings and monuments encode the Great Secret of the Ages – of all places, one would have expected *something*. A once-in-a-26,000-year event, the Mother of All Auspicious Occasions, and zip, zilch, nada.

The Year of the Grand Alignment, in the most visible Earthly counterpart of the Celestial City/Cosmic Mountain, upon which the eyes of the world are perpetually fixed, and all we get is a lousy sex scandal, spawning news stories by the thousands filled with details about the penis of the Most Powerful Man in the Kingdom/World, a cigar-as-phallus, the young lady's vagina, semen, the White House (geographic parallel to the cosmic Place of Crossing)… hey, wait a minute…

Pregnant with Meaning

The Time of Crossing at the Place of Crossing – and we find what could readily be interpreted as all the elements necessary for a modern farcical reenactment of an ancient Egyptian fertility ritual,[2] a dark comedic theatrical production based on Osirian mythology.

In one of the more popular versions of the Osiris myth, the god is killed and dismembered by his brother Set, after which Osiris' sister-wife Isis is able to locate all his body parts, except his penis. She then fashions a substitute phallus and magically inseminates herself, subsequently giving birth to Horus.

It is 1998, and as above in the heavens the sun penetrates the cosmic birth canal/vagina, the Womb of Isis, so here below tales of William Jefferson Clinton inserting a phallus of tobacco into Monica Lewinsky's dark rift begin to circulate, whereupon she becomes pregnant with scandal.

The Man from Hope subsequently argues in his grand jury testimony, "It depends on what the meaning of the word 'is' is." Is is? *Isis*. Very clever.

---

2. In one such ancient Egyptian fertility ritual, a public procession led by the Pharaoh would march down to the Nile, where nation's leader would disrobe, masturbate and ejaculate into the river, symbolically imbuing it with living-giving powers. I'm sure there's a good joke in here somewhere about Bill Clinton conducting his own private semen festival in the Oval Office… Oral Orifice… I don't know.

The Man from Hope

Hope is the thing with feathers that perches in the soul and sings the tune without the words and never stops at all.

– Emily Dickinson

Born William Jefferson Blythe III in Hope, Arkansas, Bill Clinton is a member of the Order of DeMolay Hall-of-Fame, an honor he shares with Walt Disney and John Wayne, among others. Named for Jacques de Molay, the last Grand Master of the Knights Templar, the organization is affiliated with Freemasonry though not formally a part of it.

Speaking of hope, Harpocrates was the Greek god of silence, secrets, and confidentiality, and, according to Plutarch, an embodiment of hope. Harpocrates was adapted by the Greeks from one of the most well-known Egyptian deities, and the name was rendered from the Egyptian, *Har-pa-kehered*, "Horus the Child," who represented the newborn sun, rising each day at dawn.

Bill Clinton, the Man from Hope, playing the part – for the purposes of the 1998 Galactic Alignment Dark Comedy – of Horus, sun god.

P.S.: Speaking of playing the part, Clinton made a big production about not having actually had "sexual relations" with Monica Lewinsky (according to a strict legal interpretation of the term), employing tortured logic and twisted semantics in an attempt to argue his point. Personally, I find it a little difficult to believe that Slick Willie – serial philanderer, adulterer and rapist (one might even add pedophile to this list; Google Jeffrey Epstein, Orgy Island and *The Lolita Express*), who left a trail of victims with chewed-up lips from Little Rock to D.C. – all of a sudden grew a conscience about porking an intern in the Oval Office, and I suspect that entire routine was designed to invoke the Isis-as-the-Great-Virgin meme. But I could be wrong.

Bill Clinton, Man-Ho-r-us.

SCRIPTED EVENTS

Now, even at this point in our journey, you're probably still skeptical that such events could be orchestrated on this scale or at this level. I can sympathize. Feel free to get off the ride any time you want, because if you don't like what I've just told you, you're gonna *hate* this next part...

On August 20th, 1998, three days after President Clinton testified before the grand jury in the Lewinsky scandal, a series of missiles were launched against suspected terrorist bases in Sudan and Afghanistan as part of Operation Infinite Reach. That same day had also concluded Lewinsky's second day of testimony before the grand jury, and pre-announced Special Reports on this topic were pre-empted by breaking news of the missile attacks.

Clinton was immediately accused by a variety of critics of ordering the attacks as a diversion from the negative press surrounding the sex scandal, and Operation Infinite Reach subsequently became known as "Monica's War."

Astute observers (as well as not-so-astute, because it was completely obvious) noted with some incredulity the striking parallel between this episode and the plot of the recently released movie, *Wag the Dog*, in which a spin doctor and a Hollywood producer fabricate a war in Albania in order to distract voters from a sex scandal involving the U.S. President less than two weeks before an election.

As if that weren't enough, the exact same comparison was made again in December following Operation Desert Fox in Iraq, a four-day bombing campaign that occurred at precisely the same time that the U.S. House of Representatives was conducting the impeachment hearing of President Clinton. In fact, Clinton was formally impeached on December 19th, the final day of the military operation.

The justification given for the strikes in Iraq was their failure to comply with U.N. Security Council resolutions and its interference with U.N. Special Commission inspectors, but in reality both the rationale and the impact of the operation were suspect. There were accusations of U.S. interference in the U.N. inspection process, including infiltration of the inspection teams by CIA and MI6 operatives.

Obama: Hey, I found this in the desk drawer in the Oval Office...

CHRISTMAS PRESENT

You might be thinking that, in the grand scheme of things, what does it really matter if Clinton's handlers took inspiration from a movie and bombed some third-world countries in order to change the media narrative to one more favorable to the president? Not exactly a moral stance, but point taken.

It probably wouldn't surprise you too much at this point, though, if I told you that there is a long, well-documented history of significant historical events being foreshadowed in fiction, both print and film. This was particularly true of 9/11.

At first, you may instinctually reject the notion that the Lewinsky scandal was somehow scripted in advance – and intentionally designed to correspond with a fictional narrative – like bad sushi, but that doesn't mean it's not true.

If you think it's a coincidence that the hats these two young ladies are wearing are identical, I feel sorry for you.

So, to be clear, is what I'm telling you that *Wag the Dog* was predictive programming prefiguring the attacks in Sudan, Afghanistan and Iraq, which were ostensibly intended to distract the public and the media from the Lewinsky sex scandal but actually ended up drawing more attention to them – and that the movie contained specific details later mirrored in reality, down to Monica's hat?

That's precisely what I'm telling you, and I'll go even further – not only is the above true, but all this was coordinated on a meta-level as part of the Cryptocracy's perverse Galactic Alignment Soirée, which, as you know, is all about the rebirth of the sun, kinda like Christmas; the U.S. release date, incidentally, of *Wag the Dog*.

Starr Wars: A Bridge Too Far

You know, I *could* speculate about Kenneth Starr's role in this whole affair, and ask what the significance of the *Starr Report* being released on September 11, 1998, was (although we already know that date is all about Sirius), or whether Starr's last name was in fact an insiders' reference to the Dog Star, or whether the "White Water" investigation was code for "Milky Way," or speculate about his post-Special-Counsel gig as chancellor of Baylor University in Waco, Texas, site of the slaughter of the Branch Davidians...

...but I'm not going to.

A recently-released memo shows that then-associate-counsel-to-the-independent-counsel (Kenneth Starr) and now Supreme Court Justice Brett Kavanaugh suggested a list of sexually-graphic questions to ask Bill Clinton in Clinton's grand-jury testimony about his affair with Monica Lewinsky. What goes around comes around, huh, Brett – Devil's Triangle, anyone?

"...THIS IS THE U.S.S. NIMITZ... WHERE THE HELL ARE WE?..."

Trapped outside the boundaries of time and space—
102 aircraft...6,000 men...all missing.

THE FINAL COUNTDOWN

RICHARD R. ST. JOHNS PRESENTS
KIRK DOUGLAS   MARTIN SHEEN   KATHARINE ROSS
JAMES FARENTINO
in THE BRYNA COMPANY'S PRODUCTION of
THE FINAL COUNTDOWN Starring RON O'NEAL and CHARLES DURNING as Senator Chapman
Directed by DON TAYLOR   Produced by PETER VINCENT DOUGLAS   Executive Producer RICHARD R. ST. JOHNS
Screenplay by DAVID AMBROSE & GERRY DAVIS and THOMAS HUNTER & PETER POWELL
Story by THOMAS HUNTER & PETER POWELL and DAVID AMBROSE   Director of Photography VICTOR J. KEMPER
Music by JOHN SCOTT   Associate Producer LLOYD KAUFMAN   Edited by ROBERT K. LAMBERT
Executive in Charge of Production JOHN W. HYDE   Filmed in PANAVISION® TECHNICOLOR®

CHAPTER NINETEEN

T MINUS TEN

I'm sure you're ready to get out of 1998, and the good news is that we're going to leave it for a few minutes. The bad news is we'll have to come back to it shortly. For now, we're going back to 1988 – December 21st, the winter solstice, to be exact, ten years *to the day* prior to 12/21/1998, Zero Day of Galactic Alignment Proper.

We are in Lockerbie, Scotland, watching debris from Pan Am Flight 103 rain down on the small town. The plane has been ripped apart in mid-air by a terrorist's bomb, and the resulting disaster kills all 259 aboard and 11 more on the ground. It is the deadliest aviation disaster in British history.

PLACE OF BIRTH

A couple of hundred miles from Lockerbie is Loch Ness, Scotland (and, no, I'm not about to try to tie the Loch Ness Monster in with all this). In November 1899, Aleister Crowley purchased the Boleskine House in Foyers on the shore of Loch Ness. He quickly developed a love of Scottish culture, referring to himself as the "Laird of Boleskine," and took to wearing traditional highland dress, even during visits to London.

Led Zeppelin guitarist Jimmy Page, an avid collector of Crowley memorabilia, purchased the Boleskin House in 1970.

Lockerbie is about an equal distance from Warwickshire, perhaps best known for being the birthplace of William Shakespeare, but it is also where Aleister Crowley was brought into the world.

O, REALLY?

In *9/11 as Mass Ritual*, I discussed at length the use of airplanes as sacrificial vessels, consecrated with numbers of occult power, numbers of particular importance to Aleister Crowley and within his Thelema: 11, 77, 93 and 175.

During his lifetime, Crowley was involved with many occult groups, including the Freemasons. Around 1904, he was initiated into Craft Free-masonry,[3] and his mother lodge – as recognized under the jurisdiction of the Grande Loge Nationale Française in Paris as of 1964 – is Anglo-Saxon Lodge No. 103. One-o-three.

Houses of the Un-Holy

Speaking of old houses with interesting histories, Lockerbie House (located in…) was built in 1814 for Sir William Douglas, and was inhabited by a number of members of the Douglas family through the years, including John Sholto Douglas, who became the 9th Marquess of Queensberry and is the namesake of the "Marquess of Queensberry rules" in boxing.

Douglas is also remembered as a devout atheist, as well as for his outspoken views, brutish manner and his role in the downfall of author and playwright Oscar Wilde. Douglas' third son, Lord Alfred "Bosie," was a close friend and lover of Wilde, and Queens-berry's efforts to terminate their relationship led to his famous dispute with the author.

Wilde was left bankrupt, his assets were seized and sold at auction, he was charged and convicted of gross indecency and sentenced to two years' hard labour. He subsequently went into exile in France and died shortly thereafter.

(Left) John Sholto Douglas, the 9th Marquess of Queensberry.
(Center) Oscar Wilde (Right) Epstein's "flying demon-angel."

---

3. I'm sure I don't need to remind you of the existence of the Grand Lodge of Scotland or the Ancient and Accepted Scottish Rite of Freemasonry.

Eight years after the author's death (some say due to syphilis), sculptor Jacob Epstein was chosen to carve Wilde's tomb. The sculpture was produced during what has been referred to, for obvious reasons, as Epstein's *Sun Temple* period.

The winged figure, which has been described as a "flying demon-angel," had been endowed by Epstein with unusually large testicles. As a result, the monument was declared indecent by authorities and covered with a tarp.

Eventually, the offending portion of the sculpture was covered with a bronze butterfly-shaped ornament, and the monument was unveiled in August 1914, with Aleister Crowley presiding over the ceremony. The unveiling was absent the sculptor, who was highly displeased with the alteration to his creation.

Crowley returned to Wilde's grave several weeks later and removed the butterfly cod-piece from the monument, later recalling,

> I saw that there was only one thing to be done in the interests of common decency and respect for Epstein. I detached the butterfly and put it under my waistcoat. The gate keeper did not notice how portly I had become. When I reached London, I put on evening dress and affixed the butterfly to my own person in the same way as previously to the statue, in the interests of modesty, and then marched into the Café Royal, to the delight of the assembled multitude. Epstein himself happened to be there and it was a glorious evening. By this time he had understood my motives; that I was honestly indignant at the outrage to him and determined to uphold the privileges of the artist.

One might call that a good old one-two punch.

Countdown Initiated

As is quite often the case in major airline disasters, there are a number of conspiracy theories surrounding the downing of Pan Am Flight 103 that call into question the official explanation of events.

One of the most well-known theories in this instance is put forth in a documentary film entitled, *The Maltese Double Cross–Lockerbie*, which claims that the bomb was introduced onto the aircraft by an unwitting drug mule in a CIA-protected suitcase.

The film was widely criticized by authorities, and of course it would be, but it doesn't really matter if this alternate account is true or not – or even which of the multiple existing conspiracy theories might be accurate. The truth is, there may be multiple theories which contain partially correct information, with none of them being perfectly on target.

The explanation for this? It is quite common in false flags for the perpetrators to clandestinely integrate into the operation a number of logical suspects. The result? A fog of war, endless rabbit holes down which investigators and conspiracy theorists alike disappear, never to return.

In the case of Pan Am 103, the ultimate truth being concealed doesn't concern terrorists or drugs, but rather something far bigger, involving human sacrifice and The End of the Great Age. *T minus 10 and counting.*

CHAPTER TWENTY

T Minus 111

A s promised, or threatened, we are now back in 1998. The Pan-Am-Lodge-#103-T-Minus-10 Countdown is complete (almost).

Peggy's Cove from Swissair 111 Memorial Site

We have left Lockerbie, Scotland, and are in Peggy's Cove, Nova Scotia – "New Scotland" – watching Swissair Flight 111 plunge into the waters of St. Margarets Bay roughly five miles from shore. The plane has suffered a catastrophic failure due to an electrical fire, and the resulting disaster kills all 229 aboard. It is the deadliest McDonnell Douglas MD-11 accident in aviation history.

(Left) The Swissair MD-11 in Zurich in July 1998, just months before it crashed off the coast of Nova Scotia killing all on board.

The date is September 2nd, a couple of weeks after the August 20 missile strikes in Afghanistan and Sudan, a couple of months before the attack on Iraq, and nine days before the release of the *Starr Report*.

Ah, hah, you may be thinking, *is that all you've got? Your little 10-year-countdown is off, it doesn't end on 12/21/98, it's a load of hooey.* Alright, smartass, I'm not finished.

ELEVENTY-ONE

Given the sinister nature of this whole year-long Galactic Freak Show Charade-Celebration, one could readily view the deaths of those killed in all three countries as human sacrifices. The motives behind, and timing of, each of the attacks were legitimately called into question: their impact from a military perspective was *highly* limited, if not altogether negligible (although the resulting destabilization of Saddam Hussein's government in Iraq did have some longer-term strategic value); and, as we've explored, they could well have been part of an concerted effort to distract the public's and the media's attention from an ongoing sex scandal.

However, since we have exposed the true purpose and nature of that scandal as a globally-televised Egyptian Fertility Ritual Dark Comedy Series, we can be *certain* that these related deaths were in fact part of an act of mass human sacrifice, as were the deaths of the passengers and crew of those aboard Swissair Flight 111. *How can we be sure of the latter,* you might ask? I had hoped you weren't going to make me do this....

First, I'm just going to trust that I don't need to comment on the significance of the 111 in Swissair Flight 111. Second, noting that the aircraft was an MD-11, I'm going to quickly point out, merely as a refresher, that 11x111=1221. And third, with apologies in advance, I'm going to inform you that on September 2nd, 1998, the number of days remaining until December 21st, Galactic Alignment Proper, were, to quote Bilbo Baggins, "eleventy-one" – one-hundred and eleven. 1-1-1. T-minus...

BIRDS OF A FEATHER

Now, I could stop right here, but I'm not going to, and you're not going to stop reading because you're a glutton for punishment.

Just for the hell of it, I'm going to point out that of course there were oddities and unexplained facts related to the Swissair incident that the official explanation didn't account for, and multiple conspiracy theories emerged following the tragedy. Completely unsurprising.

Several purported eyewitnesses recalled seeing what they interpreted to be a missile streaking toward the aircraft, either fired from the ground or the ocean, and some speculated that it was a missile from a U.S. Navy warship gone terribly awry.

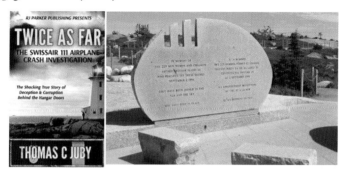

The Swissair Flight 111 Memorial in Peggy's Cove, Nova Scotia. Boy, did the designers lay an egg with this one. (Are those three notches representing 111, or twin towers?)

Then there's the matter of the $500 million worth of diamonds and jewelry that was reported to be in the cargo hold, but, although 98% of the plane's wreckage was recovered, never found. (Three days before the crash, a popular exhibition, "The Nature of Diamonds," had closed at the American Museum of National History in New York.)

Swissair Flight 111, known as the "UN Shuttle," departed from JFK International Airport, as did TWA Flight 800, which crashed into the Atlantic Ocean off the coast of New York in 1996. In this tragedy too, conspiracy theories concerning a missile, possibly fired from a U.S. Navy vessel, circulated widely. In both instances, the record of scheduled military exercises shows planned air and sea operations for the weeks of the crashes.

Despite the compelling similarities between these two cases, however, the primary point I want to make regarding TWA Flight 800, in context of our broader discussion, is this: the crash of Swissair 111 occurred exactly 777 days from the crash of TWA Flight 800… and, if for whatever reason that's not good enough for you, try this on: 800 + 111 = 911. 9-1-1. *9/11.*

Well, lookie, lookie.

Holy Shmoly

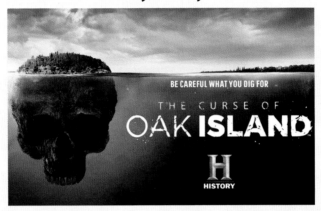

While we're on the subject of unrecovered treasure, let's note that Peggy's Cove, Novia Scotia, is less than twenty miles from the infamous Oak Island and its deadly Money Pit.

Numerous books have been published, and a number of documentaries made, about Oak Island, and unless you've been living on another planet for the last several years, you know that the *History Channel* has a series about the mystery, entitled *The Curse of Oak Island*, that's been on since 2014.

(Left) As much as I don't want to do it, I have to point out the numbers of the primary roadways leading to Oak Island and Peggy's Cove: 103 and 333. (Right) Holy shmoly, it's The Duke.

Those who have been involved with past attempts to uncover the island's secrets include Antarctic explorer Richard Byrd, John Wayne and a young Franklin D. Roosevelt, who maintained a lifelong interest in the subject.

Photograph of future U.S. President and Freemason Franklin D. Roosevelt, third from right, and others at Oak Island.

Theories about Oak Island and the Money Pit run the gamut, with a seemingly endless number of them put forward regarding the purpose of the island and the contents of the famous pit, including (as pertains to the latter):

- Marie Antoinette's jewels;

- pirate treasure buried by Captain Kidd and/or Blackbeard, who claimed that he buried his treasure "where none but Satan and myself can find it";

- original manuscripts by William Shakespeare, or whoever wrote the literary masterpieces attributed to the person of this name – some say Sir Francis Bacon might have written some or all of them; and, last but certainly not least,

- the Holy Grail and/or the Ark of the Covenant.

The list of suspects who may be responsible for the complex engineering of Oak Island's underground vault(s) and system of flood tunnels, as well as the abundant esoteric symbols and imagery discovered in numerous locations, includes, unsurprisingly, the Knights Templar and the Freemasons (or some combination thereof).

Certain elements of the Money Pit are claimed to correspond to one or more Masonic initiation rites involving the legend of Enoch and a hidden vault with a sacred treasure (Google "The Royal Arch of Enoch"), although there is some indication that the details which support this theory were fabricated. Indeed, one cannot dismiss *entirely* the possibility that the entire Oak Island legend may be an elaborate hoax perpetrated by the Freemasons.

Regardless of what the truth may be, the legend lives on, as does the memory of what occurred on September 2nd, 1998, precisely 777 days from the crash of TWA 800, and a few miles off the shore of nearby Peggy's Cove – which, incidentally, sits exactly 777 miles from the U.S. Capitol, ie. Womb of Isis.

CHARLES BARKHOUSE
EXPERT TEMPLAR

LE PRESIDENT KENNEDY
ASSASSINE A DALLAS

Il est procureur.

Il est prêt à risquer sa vie,

Celle des siens,

Tout ce qu'il a de plus cher

Pour ce qu'il a de plus sacré...

La vérité.

KEVIN COSTNER

UN FILM DE OLIVER STONE

JFK

Affaire non classée

WARNER BROS. PRÉSENTE

EN ASSOCIATION AVEC LE STUDIO CANAL+, REGENCY ENTERPRISES ET ALCOR FILMS UNE PRODUCTION IXTLAN CORPORATION ET CAMELOT HO UN FILM DE OLIVER STONE KEVIN COSTNER "JFK"
KEVIN BACON TOMMY LEE JONES LAURIE METCALF GARY OLDMAN MICHAEL ROOKER JAY O. SANDERS ET SISSY SPACEK MUSIQUE DE CLAUDIA TOWNSEND MUSIQUE DE VICTOR KEMPSTER
PHOTOGRAPHIE DE ROBERT RICHARDSON MUSIQUE DE JOHN WILLIAMS MONTAGE DE ARNON MILCHAN D'APRÈS LES LIVRES DE JIM GARRISON ET DE JIM MARRS
SCÉNARIO DE OLIVER STONE ET ZACHARY SKLAR PRODUIT PAR A. KITMAN HO ET OLIVER STONE RÉALISÉ PAR OLIVER STONE

CHAPTER TWENTY-ONE

AN AFFAIR TO REMEMBER

If, after all we've covered thus far, you're wondering whether there's any event in U.S. history that I'm *not* going to tie into this Super Conspiracy of the Ages, the answer is, Yes. Unfortunately for you, however, we haven't run out of deep connections to explore – besides, I'm not the one creating the linkages, I'm just exposing them for you. Don't blame me.

But in the interests of appearing to be sympathetic with your plight, I'm going to make this one easy on you.

START TO FINISH

My entire second book, *Most Dangerous: A True Story*, is about the assassination of President John F. Kennedy as mass ritual, and how the year 2013, the 50th anniversary of his murder, was commemorated in typically sick fashion by the Cryptocracy as the "Golden Jubilee of the Killing of the King."

Although I didn't say it this bluntly in the book, the whole damn affair in '63, front to back, top to bottom, was a Freemasonic ritual (or at the very least something posing as one), and the cover-up was orchestrated by Freemasons, including pretty-boy and future U.S. President Gerald Ford, a member of the Warren Commission and a 33° Scottish Rite Mason. He was also unanimously elected Honorary Grand Master of the International Supreme Council, Order of DeMolay, a position in which he served until January 1977.

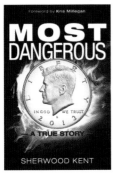

Dear Diary

Scanned from the President's Daily Diary Collection (Box 85) at the Gerald R. Ford Presidential Library

THE WHITE HOUSE				
THE DAILY DIARY OF PRESIDENT GERALD R. FORD DECLASSIFIED				

PLACE DAY BEGAN	AUTHORITY RAC nLF-PDD-1-7-4-2 1/29/08	DATE (Mo., Day, Yr.)
THE WHITE HOUSE WASHINGTON, D.C.	nsc grindstone BY /hh NARA, DATE 2/4/10	JANUARY 11, 1977
		TIME DAY 7:30 a.m. TUESDAY

TIME		PHONE	ACTIVITY
In	Out	P = Placed R = Rec'd	
11:50	12:24		The President participated in a ceremony to receive the degrees of Freemasonry from members of the Grand Chapter of Royal Arch Masons and the Grand Council of Royal and Select Master Masons of the District of Columbia. For a list of attendees, see APPENDIX "A."

During the last days of his presidency, Ford received the degrees of Freemasonry from members of the Grand Chapter of Royal Arch Masons and the Grand Council of Royal and Select Master Masons of the District of Columbia in a special ceremony in the Oval Office on January 11, 1977. That's 1/11 for the numerologically-challenged among you: 1-1-1.

Chevy Chase as President Ford on Saturday Night Live.

THE JFK ASSASSINATION AS MASS RITUAL: THE SUPER-SHORT VERSION

Fill in the blank:

I'll get you started with a freebie:

1. The typical estimate of the duration of the Great Age in years? <u>26,000</u>

2. The aircraft identification number on the tail of JFK's Air Force One: _____

3. John F. Kennedy was America's _____ [th] President.

4. JFK was assassinated in what year? _____. 1998 minus that year equals _____ years.

<u>Bonus</u>: The minimum age a person must be in order to qualify for U.S. President? ____ years old.[4]

4. Answers: #2, same as #1. #3, 35. #4, (first blank) hell everybody knows is it was 1963, which means that the second blank is the same as #3, 35 – and that's the answer to the bonus, too.

I told you I'd make this easy. I even skipped the general questions regarding the obvious aspects of the ritual – such as Dealey Plaza being the site of the first Masonic Lodge in Dallas, named for a 33rd degree Freemason and built in the shape of a trident; or, the presence of an obelisk and reflecting pool; or, as I note in my book, even the Aleister Crowley component, "R P STOVAL" in the guise of Dallas police detective R. B. Stoval (as Crowley wrote, "RPSTOVAL is the name of the Angel of the Sun, that is, the *Solar Logos of the New Aeon*" [emphasis added]).

I went straight to the questions whose answers reveal the assassination as more than an updated version of the ancient "Killing of the King" fertility ritual (although it was that) and expose it as a Galactic Alignment Countdown MegaRitual.

(Left) President Kennedy's casket being off-loaded at Andrews Airforce Base. (Right) Well, what do you know about that? The Boy from Hope meets the King of Camelot. "I David Berkowitz have been chosen since birth…"

The 35th President, assassinated in 1963, marking the commencement of a 35-year countdown to the End of the…yeah, yeah, yeah, we've heard all that before. But here's something worth considering: JFK was killed on November 22nd, 11/22. Much speculation has occurred about this fact and the obvious incorporation of these two "power numbers." I'm not going to repeat any of that here, but rather simply point out the following: 1122 would also be the numbers used to represent January 1, 2022 – 1/1/22, the First Day of the New Great Age of Satan.

I'll give you ten extra bonus points if you can tell me who the car on the left belongs to. Clue: the car on the right belonged to her alleged-white-fascist son. (11:11 and 11/22, aka 1/1/22, all in the same false flag – nice touch).

First Down and Forty to Go

Fact: the assassination of our 35th President initiated a 35-year countdown to the most precise moment of Galactic Alignment in 1998. Now, re-read these two paragraphs from an earlier chapter:

> The White House is located at 1600 Pennsylvania Avenue. If 16th Street NW didn't dead end into Lafayette Square, which sits to the immediate north of the White House, it would run directly through it. Multiplying 1600 by 16 yields 25,600, a mere 41 units short of the length of the Illuminati Great Year. Coincidence?
>
> The entire 1600 *block* of Pennsylvania Avenue represents the *window* of Galactic Alignment, which spans 40 years, give or take a little: 25,600 + 41 = 25,641. Pretty simple, and pretty plain, don't you think? (If you wanna haggle over plus or minus one year across the span of almost 26 centuries, be my guest. But keep this in mind: 25,641 can also be expressed as $4^2 \times 40^2 + 40 + 1$…very Biblical.)

All this considered, it probably won't surprise you to learn that the inauguration of our 40th president, Ronald Reagan, in 1981, initiated a 40-year countdown to the End of the Great Age in 2021.

As Reagan read his inauguration address after being sworn into office for his first term on January 20, 1981, the 52 U.S. hostages held by Iran since November 4, 1979, were released. They had been in captivity for a total of 444 days.

Besides the obvious fact of 444 being the product of 4 times 111, and the less obvious fact of 1776 being the product of 4 times 444, there is the aforementioned expression of the Great Age's Number of Completion (25,641) as $4^2 \times 40^2 + 40 + 1$. (That's a lot of fours…and here's three more: the number 1980, the year of Reagan's election, is the product of 44 times 45.) The Final Forty.

(P.S.: Maybe First Lady Nancy Reagan's obsession with horoscopes is perhaps an indication that she knew more about all this than she was letting on. Or, maybe not.)

CHAPTER TWENTY-TWO

Like Sands Through the Hourglass...

Unless I've somehow managed to be unclear about it previously, this is all about *time*. You could say that time is at the very heart of the matter – sorta like how the WWII Memorial and the Washington Monument are at the precise center of Washington, DC.

Dead Center

Washington, DC, was laid out as a 10-mile square, with boundary stones set at each of the four corners. The center of this square is approximately in the middle of the block to the immediate east of the White House Ellipse (between 17th and 18th Streets NW on Constitution Avenue), although to my knowledge there's nothing at that location to mark the spot (if you don't count the Art Museum of the Americas).

1700 feet from Jefferson Pier

The symbolic, functional center of Washington is formed by the north-south center axis of the White House and the east-west center axis of the U.S. Capitol (which is different from the geographic center of D.C., but this is irrelevant to our discussion). This mid-point is marked by the Jefferson Pier, named after Thomas Jefferson, who at the time was serving as the U.S. Secretary of State and supervising the initial planning of the nation's capital. Jefferson hoped that this would become the new "first meridian," but it obviously never did.

(Above) If Jefferson had gotten his way, the pier named after him would have marked longitude 0′ 0." (Right) The top of the Jefferson Pier.

The inscription on the Jefferson Pier reads:

> Position of Jefferson
> PIER ERECTED DEC. 18, 1804.
> RECOVERED AND RE-ERECTED
> DEC. 2, 1889.
> *[this obscured line formerly read,*
> *"BEING THE CENTER POINT OF THE"]*
> DISTRICT OF COLUMBIA

Not only did someone apparently have an issue with the fifth line and crudely chiseled it out, but at one point the marker was removed entirely and had to be re-erected at a later date.[5]

The date of Easter each year hinges upon the time of the vernal equinox, which is ecclesiastically set as March 21st, although in reality, on the Gregorian calendar it shifts over the 400-year leap-year cycle between March 19th and 21st. From the church's perspective, a calendar which kept the equinox on March 21st would be by far preferable.

"God's Chosen Meridian," as it is also been called, corresponds to the 77th meridian west (77° west of Greenwich), the meridian on which Washington, D.C., is located. Is this the reason, or one of the reasons, that Thomas Jefferson sought to establish a new Prime Meridian through the

5. Connected with John Dee's 33-year "Perfect Christian Calendar," as it has sometimes been referred to, is the concept of "God's Longitude." I'm not going into detail on the subject, because I don't know enough about it to do so, but if I understand it correctly (and I'm not entirely sure that I do, or want to), this would correspond to the meridian on which the vernal equinox fell on the same day every year using the 33-year calendar. This has various implications, in particular for the Easter holiday.

heart of Washington, D.C. – because he believed that this meridian was "God's Longitude"?

I find that an interesting prospect, but the truth is I have no idea if it's true or not, which is why I put this in a footnote. There's more to the story, including Protestant vs. Catholic intrigue, but, quite frankly, this is about as far as I care to take the discussion.

BIT OF A STRETCH

A 10-mile square bears an interesting relationship to the New Jerusalem, described in the *Book of Revelation* as a cube.

The D.C. Square measures 52,800 feet on each side, while the length of the New Jerusalem's four walls are given as 12,000 stadia each. The number 52,800 divided by 12,000 equals 4.4, although this operation obviously isn't a conversion of units. (Quite frankly, I hesitate to mention this point, and wouldn't, if not for the previously-established extreme importance of the number 44.)

Did the designers of Washington, D.C., select the dimensions of the city, at least in part, for this reason, i.e., because a 10-mile square bears this specific mathematical relationship with the dimensions of the New Jerusalem? I'd say, as you're probably thinking, that this is quite a stretch.

Although, you'll have to admit that stamping the future Capital of the Free World with Horus' special number (even a slight variation thereof) – as a direct affront to Yahweh, whose number is 26 – in order to commemorate the Aeon of Horus on the cusp of the New Great Age has a helluva lot of appeal. Horus City.

A BIG ZERO

A s discussed in a previous chapter, the White House and grounds represent the Alpha and the Omega, beginning and end, the completion of one great cycle and the start of the next. It is the terrestrial counterpart of the Celestial Great Cross, and one could also say that it represents the Center of Time.

The White House itself sits only slightly more than a half-mile due north from the Jefferson Pier, the Heart of D.C., which, like the White House, could also be said to represent the Heart of Time. The White House corresponds to ground zero of an astronomical alignment which marks the Shift of the Great Age, and the Heart of D.C. corresponds to a zero point in time (0'0"=00:00). It is a second, complimentary encoding of the Null Point, sitting a short distance due south of the Great Cross, on the White House, or 16th Street, Meridian.

As you will see, we will find multiple, over-lapping, reinforcing encodings of the same basic facts here, just as we discovered earlier that Galactic Center is symbolized by both Capitol Hill and the U.S. Capitol building – and just as it can by symbolized by a skull cap, cosmic mountain or womb.

Holy of Holies

The White House grounds represent a 40-year Window of Time, the Window of Galactic Alignment.

Could it be that the two-pair of axes – the intersection of one marking the actual center of the 10-mile square and the intersection of the other marking the Heart of D.C. as indicated by the Jefferson Pier – were intentionally offset in order to demarcate a similar, hidden window at the very center of Washington?

A *second* encoding of a Window of Time, perhaps also symbolizing (or darkly mocking) the *Sanctum Sanctorum*, the Holy of Holies, the inner sanctuary of the Tabernacle where God's presence appeared – described in the Bible as a cube, like the New Jerusalem itself?

Bear with me. If this all seems a little esoteric, or pointless even, trust me – in a few minutes, *it won't*.

Explain This

Horus City, a scale version of the New Jerusalem, with a hidden Holy of Holies at its core? If this sounds like a dark joke, perhaps it is – a permanent Black Mass embedded into the landscape. Or maybe it's all in my imagination. But if it is, you'll have to explain a few things to me.

The Heart of D.C., the Heart of Time, a Window of Time: if these are all are artifacts of an overactive mind, then why at this very location do we find two striking objects which, to the untrained eye, are merely national monuments, but to those with eyes to see, represent something far different – and *all about time*?

MONUMENTAL DISCOVERY

The Washington Monument sits a little over a hundred yards from the Jefferson Pier, the Heart of D.C. This, the world's largest obelisk, was a central element in Dan Brown's *The Lost Symbol* (which is apparently still lost, because he didn't actually reveal any hidden secrets in the book).

The End of Days – How Many?

If you'll recall, in Chapter 7, I wrote,

> The end of a Mayan age on December 21st, 2012, was more precisely held to be the completion of the *fifth* age on their calendar, each of these ages lasting approximately 5,125 years. Five of these ages would last roughly 26,000 years – or about the length of a Great Age.
>
> Was the end of the Mayan Fifth Age also the end of the Great Age, and how do we know when the Precessional Clock starts and stops? Recall from an earlier chapter that during Galactic Alignment "the sun, from our vantage point, lines up with the galactic equator near galactic center," and that this occurs once every 26,000 years.
>
> Does Galactic Alignment, then, mark the Alpha and the Omega, the end of one Great Age and the beginning of the next – and, if so, was the completion of 13 baktun on the Mayan calendar (corresponding to December 21st, 2012, on the Gregorian calendar), the precise end date of the Great Age?

The Maya developed over-lapping, inter-locking calendars tracking sets of 260, 360 and 365 days. A baktun lasted 144,000 days, thus 13 baktun equaled 1,872,000 days. This is approximately 5,125 years using a 365-day calendar, but it is precisely 5,200 years on a 360-day calendar. Five Mayan ages would thus be 9,360,000 days in duration – *exactly* 26,000 years on a 360-day calendar (which in Biblical context is referred to as a "prophetic year").

So what? It is striking and beyond coincidence that these same numbers can be found in the Book of Revelation. Recall that the length of each wall of the New Jerusalem is 12,000 stadia, and scripture also states that the width of the walls is 144 cubits. Twelve thousand multiplied by 144 equals 1,728,000 – 144,000 short of the number of days in a Mayan age.

But, wait – the walls of the city have twelve foundations. The twelve foundations multiplied by the length of each wall, 12,000, equals 144,000. The number of each of the four vertical walls is thus 1,872,000, and don't forget about the floor of the city. Five surfaces, five times 1,872,000…the number of days in the Great Age. *Time encoded as distance* (or other physical measurement): The New Jerusalem Date Cube. (Or do you really believe that Yahweh flies around in a 1,400-mile cube with walls made of jasper?)

P.S. Further tipping us off that we are dealing with a Zodiacal calendar are the gems adorning the 12 foundations of the city, which are in fact the gemstones associated with the 12 signs of the zodiac. (We won't even get into all of the other astrotheological imagery in the rest of the last chapter of the Bible.) And then there's this: the description of the New Jerusalem is found in Revelation Chapter 21, verses 12-21. Just for fun, let's all repeat: 12 x 1221 = 25641.

Mathematical Shorthand for the Apocalypse:

$$72.222\ldots \times 360 = 26,000$$
$$72.222\ldots \times 360^2 = 9,360,000$$

The monument is a massive Phallus of Osiris, and so much more. Much has been made of the height of the monument, 555.5 feet (I *knooow* that it's listed as 555' 5.125" according to the NPS's 1884 measurement, don't haggle with me), and the fact that this translates into 6,666 inches. One should also note that 555.5 is also exactly half of 1111, which we've seen before as 11:11. Potentially of even greater significance in this context is that, according to legend, the date when the nine founders of what would become the Knights Templar first assembled is 1,111 A.D. (If you want to confirm this, you can call the White House main line at 202-456-1111.)

Additionally, the distance from the southern portico of the White House to the center of the Jefferson Memorial dome is 1.11 miles: the Washington Monument sits precisely at the mid-point of this distance, .555 miles. (The length of each side of the base of the monument is 55 feet and change, and the batter or slope of the outer surface is 0.247 inches per foot, or 1°11'.)

(Left) As above, so below. 555.5 above + 555.5 below = 1111. (Center) Knights Templar. (Right) From her heel to the top of her head, the Statue of Liberty is 111'1" tall.

Starting to get the point? Good.

A STRONG FOUNDATION

In the historic architectural renderings for the Washington Monument, you will find that the original depth of the foundation for the obelisk was 23'4" feet. (The structure was initially constructed with a foundation of this depth, but it subsequently had to be deepened and reinforced to support the enormous weight of the monument.)

This is very interesting, given the role of the foundation of the New Jerusalem Date Cube, and given the "Mathematical Shorthand for the

Apocalypse" revealed at the end of the <u>sidebar</u>, because what 23.4 (I know 23'4" and 23.4' aren't exactly the same, we're not doing conversions, dammit) gives us is, in fact,

A 2nd Mathematical Shorthand for the Apocalypse:

$$23.4 \times 1111.1111\ldots = 26{,}000$$
$$23.4 \times 360 \times 1111.1111\ldots = 9{,}360{,}000$$

You'll of course have already noted with great interest (if you wet your pants, that's okay) that the key multiplier is 1111 (and some change). *The Washington Monument, designed to encode the length of the Great Age, both in prophetic years and in total number of days.* The Great Year in Stone.

And as if that weren't enough, the cornerstone for the monument was laid on July 4th (the date of the conjunction of Sirius and the sun), 1848, making it exactly 150 years old in 1998, the Year of Galactic Alignment Proper. Somebody pinch me.

MORE FUN MATH FACTS

1. As everybody knows, the Freemasons are big on the number 33. The square root of 1111.1111 (repeating) is 33.33 (repeating).

2. The height of the Washington Monument is 555.5 feet, which equals 6,666 inches: 555 + 666 = 1221.

3. $-1 + 11 + 11 \times 11 \times 111 = 25641$

KEY EVIDENCE

The second of the "striking objects" posing as a national monument sitting dead center at the Null Point of the D.C. New Jerusalem Date Cube is, of course, the World War II Memorial – both the design and location of which were roundly criticized from the outset.

This situation recalls the design of the Flight 93 Memorial in Shanksville (shank, box-cutters, get it?), Pennsylvania, concerning which I wrote the following in *9/11 as Mass Ritual*:

> According to the official government version of events, Islamic terrorists bring down Flight 93, killing all aboard … and the memori-

al designers propose a crescent-shaped design highly evocative of the Islamic crescent and named "The Crescent of Embrace." There are even claims that the Crescent of Embrace, as it was originally proposed and would have been oriented in the landscape, pointed directly to Mecca, a common practice in Islamic architecture. (One researcher has taken this concept a major step further by making a quite compelling case that the entire memorial was actually designed as the world's largest open-air mosque.)

This is either further mockery of the victims of the tragedy, or the damndest instance ever of tone-deafness and insensitivity in the design process of a major American memorial.

Now, before I proceed, keeping the above in mind, I'm going to remind you again of *where* we are – at the Heart of Time, the Center of the D.C. Date Cube, directly across the *Sanctum Sanctorum* from the Great-Age-in-Stone Obelisk – and I'm just going show you several objects and let you compare them.

The first, pictured left, is, obviously, the World War II Memorial, and the second two are antique brass clock-cabinet keys. (The other two I threw in for comparison, as well.)

A giant clock-cabinet key. At the Center of Time. That's just too good for words. Combine it with the fact that it is *supposed to be* a monument to the fallen American heroes of the Second World War, and you have one of the greatest examples ever of the slap-in-the-face, in-plain-sight, in-your-face public mockery employed by the Cryptocracy.

You can just have a field day with the inside jokes, which I'm sure the designers of the monument did here as in Shanksville: the Key to the Kingdom/City of God, the Key of David ("he that openeth, and no man shutteth; and shutteth, and no man openeth"), the Key to the Shaft of the Abyss/Bottomless Pit (Revelation)...

Revelation Chapter 9

[1] And the fifth angel sounded, and I saw a star fall from heaven unto the earth: and to him was given the key of the bottomless pit.

[2] And he opened the bottomless pit; and there arose a smoke out of the pit, as the smoke of a great furnace; and the sun and the air were darkened by reason of the smoke of the pit.

[3] And there came out of the smoke locusts upon the earth: and unto them was given power, as the *scorpions* of the earth have power.

[4] And it was commanded them that they should not hurt the grass of the earth, neither any green thing, neither any tree; but only those men which have not the seal of God in their foreheads.

[5] And to them it was given that they should not kill them, but that they should be tormented five months: and their torment was as the torment of a *scorpion*, when he striketh a man.

[6] And in those days shall men seek death, and shall not find it; and shall desire to die, and death shall flee from them.

[7] And the shapes of the locusts were like unto horses prepared unto battle; and on their heads were as it were crowns like gold, and their faces were as the faces of men.

[8] And they had hair as the hair of women, and their teeth were as the teeth of lions.

[9] And they had breastplates, as it were breastplates of iron; and the sound of their wings was as the sound of chariots of many horses running to battle.

[10] And they had tails like unto *scorpions*, and there were stings in their tails: and their power was to hurt men five months.

[11] And they had a king over them, which is the angel of the bottomless pit, whose name in the Hebrew tongue is Abaddon, but in the Greek tongue hath his name Apollyon.

Scorpions, huh? The constellation of Scorpio is one of the celestial markers for Galactic Center (it's stinger points directly at it, along with the tip of Sagittarius' arrow; "And I saw, and behold a white horse: and he that sat on him had a bow…"), which, as we know today, is home to a supermassive black hole, or bottomless pit, you might say.

Anyway, even if you're not a baby-sacrificing Satanist, you kinda gotta dig the whole key-to-unleashing-the-Scorpion-Locusts-on-the-earth thing.

HEAVENLY GATES

The design for the World War II Memorial, which is located on 17th Street NW, includes 56 pillars that are 17' above grade (we've already been over the whole 17th Tarot-The Star-Sirius bit) and are each, ahem, 4'4" wide.

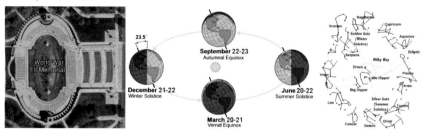

The elliptical ring inside the reflecting pool represents the Earth's elliptical orbit around the sun, and the two fountains at the north and south ends represent the Earth's position at the winter and summer solstices, respectively. Also located at the ends of the pool are two triumphal arches, the northern arch inscribed with "Atlantic" and the southern, "Pacific."

The northern arch in fact represents the Golden Gate, the Gate of God – which is the Milky Way-ecliptic crossing at the Scorpio-Sagittarius nexus – and the southern arch the Silver Gate, the Gate of Man, the Milky Way-ecliptic crossing at the Gemini-Taurus nexus (this gate was represented by the horns of Isis and the associated constellation of Taurus).

Many ancient religious traditions held that between incarnations on this planet, souls dwelled in the Milky Way. Macrobius, among others, said that during a solstice, the corresponding gate opens: souls could incarnate on Earth by descending through the Silver Gate or ascend to the heavens through the Golden Gate.

UNLOCKING SECRETS

The World War II Memorial, then, encodes most of the major elements associated with Galactic Alignment, including the winter solstice (yes, alignment can also be encoded using the summer solstice, but not in my book) and the constellations of Scorpio and Sagittarius, markers for the center of the Milky Way. It is the *key* to understanding (please hold your applause) the Grand Cycle and the End of the Great Age.

I'm sure there's some other stuff encoded in there, including something to do with 30 aethyrs, but I'm about as tired of this crap as you are, so I'm gonna stop here.

AND MILES TO GO BEFORE WE SLEEP

The 10-Mile-Square Horus City Date Matrix, with the Great Year in Stone and the World's Largest Clock-Cabinet Key at its core, sitting on God's Longitude. This already sounds like some demonic Time Machine designed to alter the course of history itself, and we're not even done examining its components and inner-workings yet.

CHAPTER TWENTY-THREE

WRITTEN IN STONE

It's a brand new chapter, and after the last one, I'll bet you were hoping that we're done with the Washington Monument. Well, we're not, because it has more to reveal to us.

We've learned that the monument and its foundation encode the Great Age, both in prophetic years and in total number of days. As we know, the Washington Monument's height is 555.5 feet, and it consists of a 500-foot tall column and a 55.5-foot tall pyramidion.

Just as half of 1111 is 555.5, half of 111 is 55.5; 55.5 times 12 is 666 (55.5'=666," very Biblical…hey, 111 *and* 666 – it's the Magic Square of the Sun!); and, 55.5 times four is 222.

A 55.5-foot-tall, four-sided pyramidion, and 55.5 multiplied by four equals 222. I'm just gonna take a stab in the dark here and say that maybe the dimensions of the pyramidion encode 222 years, the final set of 222 years in the dying Great Age – not the 222-year span from 1776 to 1998, but from 1800 to 2022. (Recall that both the White House and the U.S. Capitol entered service in 1800; also note that in numerology, you drop the zero – 2022 → 222.)

Not only that, but the pyramidion encodes the most-precise year of Galactic Alignment, 1998. How do we know all this? The pyramidion is 666" tall, the capstone 62" and the aluminum apex 8.9." (You don't have to literally multiply the height of the pyramidion or its component parts by four – the proportions involved are what encode the relevant information. Don't get all uptight on me.)

From the base of the pyramidion to the base of the capstone is 595.1," representing 198 years; and, from the base of the capstone to the tip of the apex is 70.9," representing 24 years. (Feel free to run the numbers yourself: 595.1 is 89.35% of 666, and 70.9 is 10.65%; multiply these percentages by 222 and round to the nearest whole number.)

The base of the pyramidion represents the year 1800 A.D.: 1800 plus 198 equals 1998, and 1998 plus 24 equals 222. *Party over, oops, out of time.*

A MEASURED APPROACH

Now, after all that, I know what you're thinking – *Next thing you know, he's gonna be telling us that the distance from the Washington Monument to the Capitol Dome encodes the 245 years from the founding of the New Atlantis in 1776 to the Last Year of the Dying Great Age in 2021. Right.*

That's easy enough to test:

- 245 years times 365.24 days/year equals 89,483.8 days; assuming that distance encodes time here (days = inches),

- 89,483.8 inches divided by 12 inches/foot equals 7,456.98 feet;

- 7,456.98 feet divided by 5,280 feet per mile equals 1.41 miles.

The distance from the center of the Washington Monument to the center of the Capitol Dome? 1.41 miles. Well, whattaya know about that?

CAPTAIN MIDNIGHT

Our Gigantic Magickal Sun-Calendar Stone had a couple of extra tricks up its sleeve, including the encoding of "the 245 years from the founding of the New Atlantis in 1776 to the Last Year of the Dying Great Age in 2021."

Two-hundred and forty-five years … 245 is the product of 7 and 35 (we've of course previously noted the 35-Year JFK "Killing of the King" Countdown from 1963 to 1998). Seven sets of 35, ending in 2021.

Subtracting 35 from 2021 takes us back to 1986. Anything space-related happen that year? Just the January mid-air explosion of the Space Shuttle *Challenger*, whose maiden flight began on April 4, 1983 – 4/4. Also, in April, electrical engineer John R. McDougall, using the pseudonym "Captain Midnight," committed an act of "video terrorism" by jamming the Home Box Office (HBO) signal on Hughes Communications' *Galaxy 1* satellite during a showing of the film, *The Falcon and the Snowman* (44, Galaxy, Falcon …). The Final 35?

GEOMETRIC TRUTH

More to the point here is that the prime factorization of 245 *is/yields* 5, 7 and 7. Why is this significant?

-Let's play "Why Are All These Alike?"-

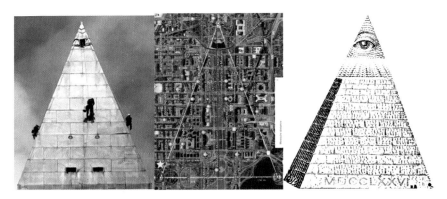

Look closely at the three pyramids pictured above.

- The first is obviously the pyramidion atop the Washington Monument.
- The second is a triangle formed by the Capitol Dome, White House and Jefferson Memorial.
- The third, as I'm sure you recognize, is the unfinished pyramid and Eye of Providence in the Great Seal of the United States on the reverse of the one-dollar bill.

The four-sided pyramidion consists of 13 levels, including the capstone, and one could view it as being projected in two dimensions from atop the monument onto the National Mall in front of it. This triangle, too, has 13 levels (formed by cross streets), including a "capstone," at the tip of which sits the Capitol Dome/Womb of Isis. The dollar-bill pyramid has 13 levels, as well – but there are 13s all over the Great Seal, and most everybody knows that 13 is a major number in the occult (as well as the original number of U.S. colonies), so I'm not going to say much else about it.

The numbers we're interested in here are 5 and 7, in particular because each of the three pyramids pictured is a 5-7-7 acute isosceles triangle. The number 245 can be expressed as 7x35, or 5x49, or $5x7^2$, or, 5x7x7. 5-7-7.

Each of these three triangles, then, encodes the 245-year countdown from 1776 to 2021. This means that the pyramidion encodes the 222 years from 1800 to 2022 and the 245 years beginning in 1776 – and it also means that the National Mall pyramid encodes 245 years twice: in the 5-7-7 pyramid and in the distance from the Washington Monument to the Capitol Dome.

Zip-A-Dee-Doo-Dah, Part II

We're all gonna have so much f*cking fun we're gonna need plastic surgery to remove our g*ddamn smiles! You'll be whistling 'Zip-A-Dee Doo-Dah' out of you're a**holes!
– Chevy Chase as Clark W. Griswold in National Lampoon's *Vacation*

Recall from an earlier chapter the propititious location of zip code 20220 directly adjacent to the White House, where it ceremoniously denotes the year 2022, and ask yourself the following question: *If he's right about all this, and 2021 is The End, and the distance from the Washington Monument encodes the 245 years from 1776 to 2021, where should we expect to find zip code 20210?*

Yep, of all the places in the Big Ole U.S.A., zip code 20210 is directly adjacent to the U.S. Capitol. (If you even *think* the word "coincidence," I'm gonna punch you in the head.)

YULE LOG

Incidentally, the London Bombings on July 7, 2005, occurred 17 years prior to 2022, and we know the significance of 17. Hmmm, 7/7/5…

In any case, as we've noted, 245 is the product of 5×7^2. Five times 245 is 1225, or $5^2 \times 7^2$, or 35^2. December 25, 2021, or 12/25/21, will technically be the First Dawn Rising of the New Sun of the Next Great Age – although, as we know, our good friends don't worship the sun, they worship Sirius, so they're not gonna do anything to commemorate it (other than this numerological stuff we just looked at). Merry Christmas.

CHAPTER TWENTY-FOUR

TEDDY, BARE(D)

"Death had to take Roosevelt sleeping, for if he had been awake, there would have been a fight."
– Thomas R. Marshall, U.S. Vice-President under Theodore Roosevelt, upon learning of the President's passing during the night.

About a mile and a half west of the White House, in the Potomac River, is Theodore Roosevelt Island (formerly known as "Mason's Island"), named of course for our 26th President, one of fourteen occupants of said house who were Freemasons.

Roosevelt joined the Freemasons and was raised to the rank of Master Mason in 1901, the year he began his service as President, less than 12 months before the assassination of President McKinley. (McKinley was a fellow Freemason…maybe he forgot to pay his membership dues.)

Roosevelt's mother lodge was located in his hometown of Oyster Bay, New York, and as President he visited numerous Masonic Lodges during his travels across the country and around the world. He also attended many Masonic ceremonies, including cornerstone layings and ground breakings. In 1902, he gave a speech at the Grand Lodge of Pennsylvania's 150th anniversary celebration of George Washington's initiation.

On April 4, 1904 – 4/4/4 – the Pentalpha Lodge No. 23 in Washington, D.C. made him an honorary member.

GETTING THE MESSAGE ACROSS

The primary feature of Theodore Roosevelt Island is the picturesque Memorial Plaza, pictured above.

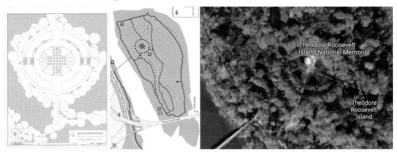

(Left) The design of the plaza. (Center) The orientation of the plaza in the landscape.

As you can see, the plaza is not oriented north-south, but rather at an angle. Why would it not be aligned with the cardinal directions and the solstitial and equinoctial axes? Is there a message here?

You know there is.

The center of the plaza is located due west of the southern portico of the White House, and I don't need to remind you that The Most Famous Residence in the World represents the Great Galactic Cross. The White House and grounds are of course oriented north-south, and we've already covered how Galactic Alignment is encoded there.

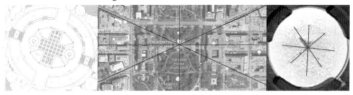

(Right) Aerial view of the fountain on the south lawn of the White House.

The angled orientation of the Theodore Roosevelt Island National Memorial, as the plaza is also known, is intended to convey that the configuration is designed to symbolize something other than the usual solstitial-equinoctial solar alignment that many such designs incorporate – and you can guess what that is…Galactic Alignment.

That same message – "this ain't about north-south-east-west" – is conveyed, or reinforced, on the White House grounds by the arms of the off-angle "compass" on the bottom of the fountain on the South Lawn (pictured above right).

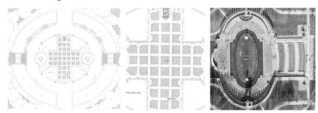

The design of the plaza shares some similarities with the World War II Giant Clock-Cabinet Key, but there are significant differences, including the Triple Cross at the center.

Also, in contrast with the WWII Memorial, the two fountains representing the earth's positions in its elliptical orbit around the sun are positioned not at the solstitial points, but at the equinoctial points. So, this is not, in fact, a reference to Galactic Alignment?

The equinox-solstice cross aligns with the Galactic Cross circa 2012.

To the contrary, it is very much so – it is a second way of encoding exactly the same alignment. The solstice-galaxy alignment and the equinox-galaxy cross, found here, refer to the same event.

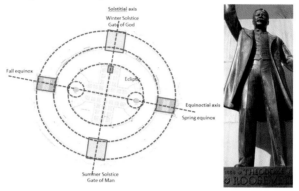

You'll note that, as with the WWII Memorial, the Gate of God is oriented at the top (which is entirely appropriate) … and what is standing directly in front of that gate – but a larger-than-life likeness of our 26th President.

Teddy Roosevelt as God? Some historians might argue so, but there's a different message here.

We already know all too well that all of this is about "As above, so below" in a major way. This whole Grand Occasion is centered on the Great Cross, which I've pointed out repeatedly is represented in the Celestial City of Washington, D.C., by the White House. And, well, well, here's Big Ole Teddy, due west of his former residence, striking the classic as-above-so-below pose (no, he's not just gesticulating), blatantly reinforcing the central message.

Stone-Cold Teddy

Congress authorized the Mount Rushmore National Memorial Commission on March 3 – 3/3 – 1925, and in 1933, the National Park Service took Mount Rushmore under its jurisdiction.

Let's see, what do we have here? George Washington, Freemason. Thomas Jefferson, maybe a Freemason, buddies with lots of famous Freemasons. Teddy Roosevelt, Freemason. Across the gap there, all by himself, Abraham Lincoln, *not* a Freemason (and most likely assassinated by Freemasons, or the very-likely-Masonic-linked Knights of the Golden Circle, with investigations into the assassination almost assuredly being muddied up by high-level Freemasons. The sculptors in charge of the Mount Rushmore project were Gutzon and Lincoln Borglum, father and son, also Freemasons.)

Excerpt from, "Thomas Jefferson: Freemason or Not?"[1]

The question of whether or not Thomas Jefferson was a Mason has been argued for two hundred years. Most Masonic scholars take the position that he was not a Mason because there is no contemporary evidence that he ever belonged to a lodge of Freemasons. Most of the claims of his membership are based on his close associations with so many other Masons: George Washington, Benjamin Franklin, John Paul Jones, James Monroe, Lewis Meriwether, William Clark, and Voltaire.

However, there is some evidence that indicates he may have been a Mason and that he attended Masonic meetings. Dr. Joseph Guillotin reported that he attended meetings at the prestigious Lodge of Nine Muses in Paris, France – the same lodge attended by Voltaire, Benjamin Franklin, and John Paul Jones. He marched in a Masonic procession with Widow's Son Lodge No. 60 and Charlottesville Lodge No. 90 on October 6, 1817, and participated in laying the cornerstone for Central College (now known as the University of Virginia.) In 1801, twenty-five years prior to his death, a lodge was chartered in Surry Court House, Virginia – it was named Jefferson Lodge No. 65. And most notably, upon his death on *July 4* [emphasis added], 1826, both the Grand Lodge of South Carolina and the Grand Lodge of Louisiana held Masonic funeral rites and processions for him. ...

If he wasn't a Mason, he clearly possessed all the prerequisites for membership, and his beliefs, his philosophies, and his great skill in architecture were certainly indicative of Masonic affiliation. But he took the answer to that question to his grave – a big obelisk he designed himself. Odd, huh?

---

1. http://www.midnightfreemasons.org/2011/10/thomas-jefferson-freemason-or-not_21.html

(Left) This is Teddy Roosevelt giving a speech. (Center) This is not Teddy Roosevelt giving a speech. (Right) Can I get a witness? Thanks, George.

Can I get a second witness? Thanks, Jack. (Pictured: The doctored photograph that was the final image from Stanley Kubrick's The Shining.*)*

Which of these is scariest?

I made this.

CHAPTER TWENTY-FIVE

ABRAHAM LINCOLN'S TEMPLE OF DOOM

I n the last chapter, I stated that Abraham Lincoln was "most likely assassinated by Freemasons, or the very-likely-Masonic-linked Knights of the Golden Circle, with investigations into the assassination almost assuredly being muddied up by high-level Freemasons."

I based this statement on research I did for my second book, in which I wrote,

> Following Lincoln's assassination, a number of conspiracy theories emerged claiming the involvement of a range of powerful interests, including the Freemasons and the Rothschilds, and the supposed motives – related to everything from the Civil War to monetary policy – were as varied as the alleged conspirators, much as with the JFK assassination.
>
> At the time, there were certainly indications and allegations of Masonic involvement in Lincoln's assassination and in what many

believed to be a major cover-up that followed the killing, and it is unquestionable that high-level Freemasons were swirling all about, just as with JFK.

I noted that "John Wilkes Booth was a known member of the Knights of the Golden Circle (KGC), a pro-slavery secret society with some fairly grandiose strategic and political objectives that included annexing large portions of Mexico and South America," and that "some researchers assert that Booth was also a 33rd degree Freemason."

I further observed that Lincoln's assassination had occurred on Good Friday, which smacked of "the same black humor and sacrilege that was smeared all over the Kennedy assassination."

SITTING IN JUDGMENT

Based on the above, I would suggest, and this is just my opinion of course, that the Lincoln Memorial enshrines our 16th President not as the Great Emancipator, but rather as a top Masonic kill: Abraham Lincoln's Temple of Doom.

Whether or not that is actually the case, you have to admit that, as visually impressive as the memorial may be, it's a bit odd for the oversized likeness of Lincoln to be sitting in a structure that is not only clearly a temple, but one that bears remarkable similarities with the Temple of Zeus to boot. I've always been under the general impression that temples were built to honor gods and goddesses.

(Left) The Temple of Zeus. (Right) The Temple of Lincoln.

Speaking of which, if not a New-World Temple of Zeus with Lincoln as a stand-in (or sit-in) for the deity, then perhaps what we have is outright blasphemy, with Lincoln as Yahwey, a bearded white giant sitting upon his throne.

> And I saw a great white throne, and him that sat on it, from whose face the earth and the heaven fled away; and there was found no place for them. Revelation 20:11

Okay, who's been naughty and who's been nice? Oh, wrong myth.

The Great White Judgment Throne at the End of Time. And if you think that's funny, try this on:

Revelation 4:6 reads, "Before the throne there was as it were a sea of glass, like crystal." A "sea of glass" – you know, like a reflecting pool, as in the Lincoln Memorial Reflecting Pool, which just happens to butt up against the Giant Clock-Cabinet Key at the Center of Time.

But that's not even the best part. The Lincoln Memorial was dedicated in 1922 and will be 100-years-old in 2022. (It's also 99-feet tall, 99 being the product of 3 times 33, and 1922 plus 99 equaling 2021, the End of the Old Great Age.) Tick-tock.

OUT NUMBERED

If not a replica of the Temple of Zeus, or a mock fulfillment of Biblical prophecy with Yahweh's End-of-Days Judgment Throne, how about the House of Horus with 44-foot-tall exterior columns, each composed of 12 sections of 44 inches each – or the Seat of Satan, with his Throne Room constructed of 666s?[1]

And if all that's not good enough for you, then maybe this will be – the distance from the Lincoln Memorial to the dome of the U.S. Capitol? Exactly 2.22 miles.

Did I mention that the Washington Monument, which is what Super-size Lincoln is looking directly at, is 555.5 feet tall?

Yeah, that's probably about all my thoughts are worth.

---

1. The memorial's central chamber, housing the statue, is 4,440 square feet: 4,440 equals 666 times 6.66 (repeating). It is 60-feet tall: 4,440 x 60 = 266,400, which equals 666 x 400. The columns in the chamber are 50-feet tall and 5.5 feet across at their base: 50 + 5.5 equals 55.5, which multiplied by 12 is, as we already know, 666.

129

Smothered in 222s

We all know what 222 is about, so I'm not going to belabor the point. But it may be worth noting that in English gematria, 222 is the value of the words hell, hades and flame (and, apparently, Falco).

We've seen so many 222s I've lost count, as well as the will to count, but whatever the current total, add the following to it. In addition to 2.22 miles being the distance from Lincoln's Temple of Doom to the Womb of Isis, it is also the distance from (any guesses before I list them?):

- The House of the Temple – which is the headquarters of the Scottish Rite of Freemasonry, Southern Jurisdiction (officially, "Home of The Supreme Council, 33°, Ancient & Accepted Scottish Rite of Freemasonry, Southern Jurisdiction, Washington D.C., U.S.A.)[1] – to the Jefferson Memorial (dedicated, obviously, to Thomas Jefferson, who, as we've discussed, may or may not have been a Freemason…I'm kinda thinkin' that this is an argument in favor this notion);

- The House of the Temple to the Capitol Dome; and,

- the Pentagon to the White House.

(Left) The House of the Temple. (Center) Stained glass window in the temple. (Right) The Pentagon.

Using the mid-point of the southwest face of the Pentagon, draw a line through the northeast corner – this line takes you directly to the south portico of the White House, at a distance of 2.22 miles.

1. We noted earlier that it is 1.11 miles from the White House to the Jefferson Memorial; with a total distance of 2.22 miles from the House of the Temple to the Jefferson Memorial, it is thus 1.11 miles from the White House to the House of the Temple, as well.

Speaking of the Pentagon, in *9/11 as Mass Ritual,* I devoted an entire chapter to this unique building, including the following section:

Gimme Five: The House of Death

As has been far more than duly noted, occultists believe that numbers contain inherent spiritual and temporal power, and that to launch a plan without incorporating the proper occult power numbers could doom the plan to failure.

The Pentagon is a 5-sided building, with 5 concentric rings and 5 above-ground floors (5-5-5), and a 5-acre central plaza … modern occultists hold 5 to be the Number of Death, and the number five is sacred to the Illuminati, of which there were five founders.

In basic terms, the number five symbolizes the five points of the pentagram and all that it connotes – death, in particular, in this instance. Some occultists would contend that the greatest intensification of a number of power is its triplicate, with 555 thus yielding "Highest Death"; the U.S. Military may disagree slightly with this interpretation, however, as the rank of their most senior operational commanders is that of "five-star" (five 5-pointed stars).

So, as many would argue is the case even without reference to five as the number of death, the Pentagon is a House of Death (or, if you take this line of reasoning to its logical extent, The House of Highest Death, and who could really argue with that)…

Smothered in 5s.

In the middle of the Pentagon's 5-acre central plaza is a pentagon-shaped structure known as "Café Ground Zero," atop which sits a wooden owl.

POSTSCRIPT

Although there are dozens and dozens of eternal flames around the world, the John F. Kennedy Eternal Flame in Arlington National Cemetery is special for a variety of reasons.

Jacqueline Kennedy requested an eternal flame for her husband's grave and drew inspiration from a number of sources, including the fantasy novel *The Candle in the Wind*, the fourth book in *The Once and Future King* series by British author T. H. White. The last two books of this series were largely the basis for the 1960 stage musical *Camelot*, the cast recording of which was a favorite of the Kennedys.

Lit by Jacqueline Kennedy on November 25, 1963, during Kennedy's funeral, the flame was placed in direct line of sight with the Lincoln Memorial, which, as I've suggested, "enshrines our 16th President not as the Great Emancipator, but rather as a top Masonic kill."

As we've previously considered, JFK was also most likely "a top Masonic kill," if not the top. Unfortunately, the JFK Eternal Flame is not 2.22 miles from the Lincoln Memorial, so we can't add it to the list of buildings and monuments "smothered in 222s." However, the distance between the two is 1.28 miles, the equivalent of 222 years, so it gets an honorable mention (using our standard formula, 1.28 miles x 5,280 feet/mile x 12 inches/foot = 81,100.8 inches; inches=days, divided by 365.24 equals 222 years).

Another reason that this particular eternal flame is special is because it could be viewed as a claim of responsibility for the assassination itself (I know Jacqueline requested that it be a permanent feature of JFK's grave – there's a much deeper story here that's well beyond the scope of this book).

The Eternal Flame – and its cousin, the Torch of Liberty – is an oft-used symbol within Freemasonry, as well as a primary signature of the Illuminati, exoterically representing the inextinguishable divine spark within all humanity, and esoterically representing the flames in which the phoenix, symbolizing Lucifer, is consumed, later to be resurrected out of the ashes. The Light of Lucifer.

(Left) The Jacqueline Kennedy Garden. (Center) The Flame of Liberty in Paris, with the Eiffel Tower in the background. Completed in 1987, the sculpture is a full-sized, gold-leaf-covered replica of the Statue of Liberty's torch. The monument is located near the northern end of the Pont de l'Alma (road bridge), directly above the tunnel in which Diana, Princess of Wales, was killed-murdered-sacrificed in a fatal car crash in 1997. The Flame of Liberty subsequently became an unofficial memorial to Diana. Of course it did. (Far Right) Diana of Versailles in the Louvre Museum, Paris.

Speaking of Jacqueline, the White House garden south of the East Colonnade is named for her, and, wouldn't you know it, the distance from the John F. Kennedy Eternal Flame to the northeastern corner of the Jacqueline Kennedy Garden is...drumroll, please... 2.22 miles.

I guess we can add this one to the list of D.C. landmarks smothered in 222s, after all.

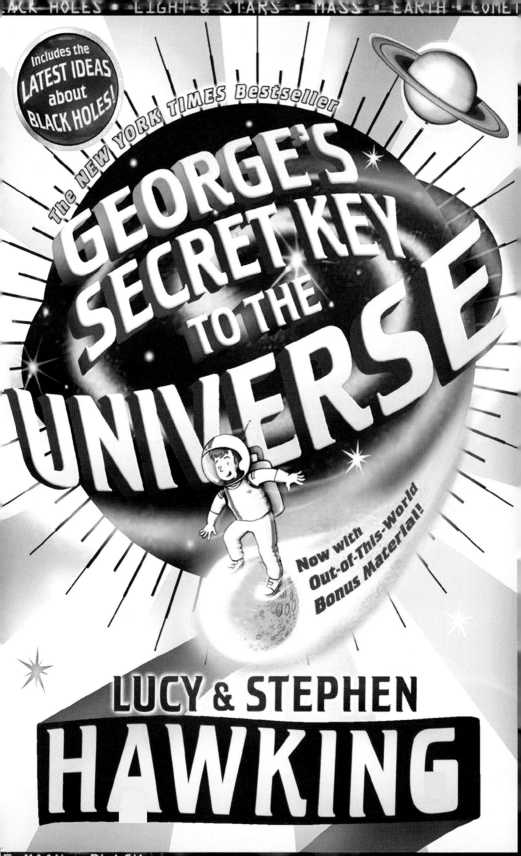

The NEW YORK TIMES Bestseller

GEORGE'S SECRET KEY TO THE UNIVERSE

Now with Out-of-This-World Bonus Material!

LUCY & STEPHEN HAWKING

CHAPTER TWENTY-SIX

GEORGE W.'S HOUSE OF LIGHT

N ot to be outdone by Abraham Lincoln's Temple of Doom or Theodore Roosevelt's Equinoctial Galactic Cross, our first President weighs in on the occult-monument scale with the George Washington National Masonic Memorial in Alexandria, Virginia, the city where I lived while working in Washington, D.C. (but who cares?).

(Left, Center) The George Washington National Masonic Memorial. (Right) The memorial is fashioned after the ancient Lighthouse of Alexandria in Egypt.

The George Washington Masonic National Memorial Association was established in 1910, meaning that it will be 111 years old in 2021 (The End of the You-Know-What), and construction started on the memorial in the same year that the Lincoln Memorial was dedicated, 1922. The height of the monument is 333 feet, and the thickness of its base is 3.33 feet.

Keeping that last point in mind, and recalling that 1,111 is basically the product of 33.33 times itself, check this out: the distance from the southern portico of the White House to the Washington National Masonic Memorial is equivalent to 1,111 years (multiply 6.404 miles times 5280 feet/mile times 12 inches/foot yields the total number of inches; inches are equivalent to days, divide by 365.242 and this equals 1,111. Again, feel free to call the White House main line at 202-456-1111 if you want to confirm this).

(Left, Center) The original "George W." in full Masonic regalia – take that, Teddy, with ya cryptic little pose – inside the George Washington Lighthouse of Alexandria, VA. (Right) So that's where the Ark of the Covenant is. (Far Right) The House of Light.

Ah, hah, you're thinking, *but this monument lies just outside the boundaries of the 10-Mile New Jerusalem Square – you can't count it!* I used to drive by the memorial all the time, it's my book, and I'll include it if I want to.

CHAPTER TWENTY-SEVEN

(THE) GREAT WORK

J ust when you thought you'd seen it all, and for sure had about as much of this junk as you could stand, here comes something even worse. I am now going to show you things you really don't want to see. We've been playing peep show, and it's time to get down to business.

THE CONJURING

I am fully aware that, over the decades, there have been many, many conspiracy-minded folk who, like myself, had too much time on their hands and found, or think they did, everything under the sun encoded in the streets of Washington, D.C. I get that. I also know that, at times, I can have an overactive imagination, and, as a very visually-oriented person, can see things that may or may not be real (I haven't started hallucinating...yet...I don't think).

I also know that the uber-elite, mega-wealthy, black-magic-lovin' maniacal geniuses who have methodically constructed The Most Powerful City on Earth over the past two centuries went absolutely bananas with encoded symbols in this extremely-important geographic location.

I'm not talking about an inverted pentagram here or there. I'm talking about a whole slew of symbols – occult, alchemical – overlapping, interlocking symbols. Very specific symbols with very specific meanings, that, when employed in certain combinations, under the correct circumstances, constitute magickal workings.

And it doesn't matter whether you believe in this type of thing or not – the super-elite that built D.C. and run this world *do*, at least on some level (even if they aren't *true* believers or aren't really concerned with anything but advancing their own interests and accruing more power). The results are what matter.

I'm not talking about mere occult graffiti. I'm talking about symbolic programming of our environment and our consciousness. Spell-casting on a monumental scale, across monumental time. The intent is to conjure dark forces that sit outside our space and time, and, so it is believed, when these forces enter into our existence, they fundamentally alter it in profound ways, and almost never to the benefit of the general populace.

ENOUGH ALREADY

We've already talked about the major encodings, the Galactic-Alignment and Great-Age-in-Stone stuff (although we're not done on that subject, either). We've looked at the 10-Mile D.C. Square, House of the Sun, Dome of Isis, House of the Temple, Zero Milestone, Clock Cabinet Key, Jefferson Pier (and Monument), auspicious dates (and zip codes), as well as Teddy's Island, Abraham's Temple, George's Lighthouse, and numerology out the wazoo.

Some conspiracy theorists also claim that there are multiple hexagrams and one or more Templar (or Maltese) Crosses incorporated into the street layout of Washington, D.C. Of this, I will only say that certain possibilities exist, but determining their validity is not essential to our current discussion, and those things we must deal with are head-splitting enough.

The National Mall as Gigantic Freemasonic Trestle Board – Or, Alchemical Symbolism for Dummies

(Left) Three Freemasonic trestle boards. (Right) You've seen this before: it's the Owl of Minerva-Moloch in the landscaping around the U.S. Capitol. It's really there – if you can't accept this, especially after everything we've covered in this book, I wouldn't recommend reading the rest of this chapter.

I'm not going to say much about this at the beginning here – just follow along, and keep in mind that I haven't steered you wrong yet (intentionally). This is ultimately a game, (I think, although a rather large one) – so don't take it too seriously.

There are a few rules, design rules, if you will:

> Rule #1:
> You are allowed one, in some instances two, missing line segments when constructing an object: they can be inferred.

> Rule #2:
> You can mirror an element, up to half of an object.

These are part of the established Freemasonic visual-language protocol utilized on the National Mall and in the street layout of Washington, D.C. – otherwise known as "not making something too damn obvious." It does *not* mean that you can make up stuff willy-nilly all over the place (something you're more than likely going to accuse me of here very shortly).

You've *Got* To Be Kidding...

Before you read the first word on this one, just looking at the images. I know you're thinking – *There's no way*. Believe me, I can sympathize. That's what I thought at first, too, and it took a while to convince myself that this could even be a possibility.

Why would they do something this big, on this scale?, I pondered. The answer is, of course, Because they can. And the worst part is, this isn't even the largest object they've encoded into the landscape, but that's the subject of the next chapter

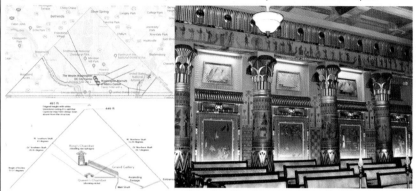

(Right) The Egyptian Hall in the Pennsylvania Grand Lodge in Philadelphia.[1]

The Great Pyramid of Giza… It would be difficult to underestimate the extent of the influence that Egyptian religion and mysticism had on the foundations of Freemasonry. Early Masonic Egyptophiles in some cases claimed to have drawn their practices and traditions from secret Egyptian texts, and in others asserted an unbroken lineage tracing all the way back to the Egyptian priesthoods.

And there is no more important symbol, or one more varied in its application or more diffused throughout the entirety of Freemasonic tradition, than the triangle. As far as rationale and motivation goes for integrating this particular symbol into the street design of the nation's capital, that's a no-brainer.

(Left) The All-Seeing Eye. The Illuminati are kinda fond of the triangle, too.

Still seem a little sketchy to you? It did to me, too – that's why I painstakingly mapped it out in detail, and to my dismay, I proved this little theory to my general satisfaction rather than disproving it. In this scheme, what is most intriguing, and perhaps convincing, is that the location of the Queen's chamber is *directly* above the White House: the floor of the chamber is the northern boundary of Lafayette Square. As significantly, the Freemasonic House of the Temple sits at the northeast tip of the floor of the King's Chamber.

Further, in this scenario, the location of the Pentagon corresponds with the pyramid's subterranean chamber, a feature some researchers hold to represent the Underworld, which would of course be a highly fitting metaphor for the headquarters of the United States Department of Defense. (Ground was broken on the construction

1. http://www.spiritualwarfareschool.com/freemasons.htm

of the Pentagon on September 11, 1941, sixty years *to the day* before it was ostensibly struck by American Airlines 77.)

I'm highly inclined to believe that these correspondences are beyond coincidence, but, if you're still not, that's okay, because what the hell does it really matter to folks like us anyway?

I did this for my benefit, not yours, but I'm showing it to you anyway (20% original size).

𝕸𝖆𝖌𝖎𝖈 𝕶𝖎𝖓𝖌𝖉𝖔𝖒

Here we go:

(Left) The Jefferson Memorial and surrounding landscape. (Center, Right) Split image.

141

(Left) Left half combined with mirrored left half. (Right) Right half horizontally flipped, then mirrored.

Two symbols for the price of one: double-winged flying sun disks. (Actually, one is an alchemical winged sun disk and the other is a flying sun disk. There's a difference.)

(Left) Winged alchemical sun. (Center) Some cheap-ass jewelry (pardon the heart shape, this was the closest thing I could find to what I was looking for). (Right) Egyptian winged sun disk.

Next, here's the same trick, except with winged alchemical eggs:

(Left) Aerial photograph of the Washington Monument. (Center) Large oval. (Right) Smaller oval.

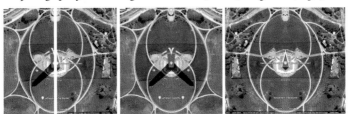

(Left) Split image. (Center) Left half combined with mirrored left half. (Right) Right half combined with mirrored right half.

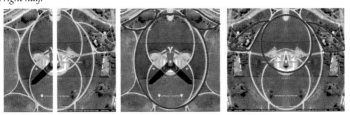

(Left) Split image. (Center) First winged egg. (Right) Second winged egg.

Two for the price of one, again. But we're not finished.

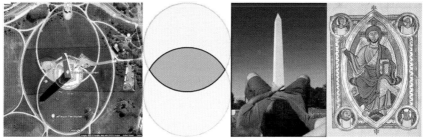

(Left) The two smaller overlapping ovals create a vesica piscis. (Next) The vesica piscis, which represents the vagina. Note that the Washington Monument is directly in the center of the vesica piscis, representing sexual union and regeneration.

And, there's more…

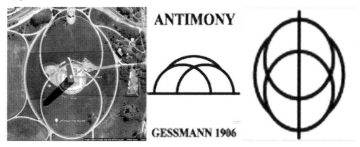

The union of all three of the ovals creates a double conjoined alchemical symbol for antimony.

Now, I couldn't tell you for certain what all this shit means if someone had a gun to my head (but that won't stop me from speculating at length, which I do in the next section). I imagine this monstrous conglomeration of symbols represents some sort of super-sized demonic sigil or talisman, or perhaps some nasty spell – or all of the above.

Whether or not this is true – and if so, whether or not anyone believes it actually works – I have no idea. My instincts tell me that, ultimately, it was the result of very powerful people having quite a bit of fun. But, then again, these are the type of people that consider ritual murder fun.

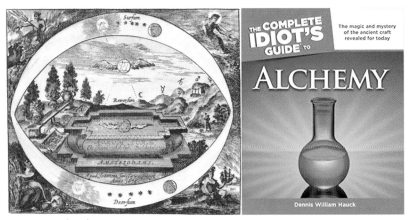

(Left) I don't know what the hell this means, either, but I like it.

Going for (Alchemical) Gold

We already know that the Washington Monument is The Great Year in Stone at the Center of Time, and encodes the Final 222, as well as working in conjunction with the Capitol Dome to encode the Final 245. It sits within an alchemical egg nested within a larger alchemical egg, and simultaneously within a vesica piscis – *and* two conjoined alchemical symbols for antimony.

I suspect that all this egg and vagina symbolism serves to reinforce the primary message of the birth of a new sun and a new cycle of time, extending these themes into metaphysical territory involving the alchemical sun and other esoteric concepts that somebody smarter than me is going to have to figure out and explain to you.

For all I know, the grounds of the National Mall contain a complete alchemical treatise sufficient for producing the fabled Philosopher's Stone and unlocking the secrets of immortality.

A Closer Look

Regarding the possible presence of a "complete alchemical treatise" and other alchemical symbols on the National Mall or in its environs, I shall say little else (primarily because I'm not qualified to do so).

However, keeping in mind the established symbolic, numerological and time-keeping significance of the Washington Monument, and the fact that it is apparently surrounded on all sides by overlapping alchemical symbols, turn your attention for a moment to another of our key symbolic structures, the White House.

I'm not going to re-hash all that the building and grounds represent in terms of Galactic Alignment, and I'm not going to tell you what I think I see in the landscape here in terms of alchemical symbolism. I'm simply going to lay it all out for you to look at. If you don't see anything, it's not going to hurt my feelings.

Just keep in mind what they did around the Jefferson Memorial and Washington Monument, and then study the images below (and for God's sake, don't take this stuff too seriously).

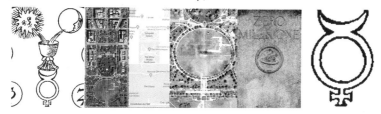

Also, and not that I'm trying to unduly influence you, keep in mind that the Zero Milestone is located at the top of The Ellipse and features Mercury's winged helmet. Speaking of Mercury, you'll of course recall his symbol there on the far right.

Now, again, I'm not attempting to lead you here, but if

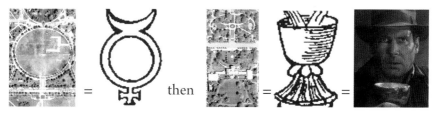

No? Well, at least you can't argue against the White House being the Holy Grail of politics.

Okay, let's try this again coming from the opposite direction.

(Left) The Haupt Fountains at the southern end of the White House grounds. Hmm, they sorta look like snake eyes to me. (Right) Lafayette Sigil-of-the-Sun Square doubling as a weird-ass esoteric plant?

145

No? Oh, well. Wait, what's that at the southern end of The Ellipse?

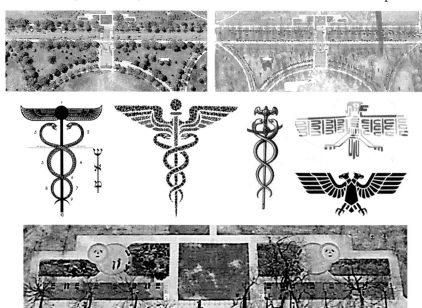

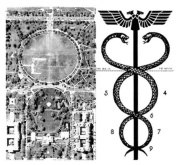

A bird's-eye view of the German-American Friendship Garden, directly across from the Haupt Fountains. Speaking of birds' eyes... right across the street from snake eyes.

(Left) The double-headed eagle of alchemy, times two. (Right) The double-headed eagle of Freemasonry.

The winged caduceus of Hermes-aka-Mercury combined with the alchemical double-headed eagle. Nice.

What? I didn't say anything.

Let's not have any vitriol over this V.I.T.R.I.O.L. (Visita Interiora Terrae Rectificando Invenies Occultum Lapidem).

But here's what I was thinking: the White House and grounds, the veritable Window of Galactic Alignment at the Center of Time, covered top to bottom, and bottom to top, with alchemical symbols – and the White House itself, the House of the Rising Sun of the New Great Age, as the stem of the alchemical chalice, the Holy Grail.

Alchemical eggs incubating in an alchemical flask, surrounded by antimony, with the World's Largest Clock-Cabinet Key doubling as the Largest Bottle Stopper in History? Now that's funny, I don't care who you are.

Most Likely My Imagination

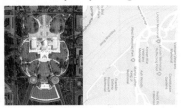

Here's our little buddy again, the Owl of Moloch, at the east end of the National Mall. Now, take a look at the west end. (Keep in mind the Mirror Rule.)
Here are a few hints:

Owl, moth (symbol of death), whatever.

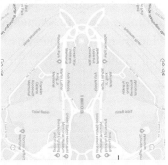

I tell you I can visualize it all
This couldn't be a dream for too real it all seems
[Chorus]
But it was just my imagination once again runnin' away with me
Tell you it was just my imagination runnin' away with me

Isn't that the Golden Snitch from Harry Potter?

CHAPTER TWENTY-EIGHT

WHEN YOU WISH UPON A STAR...

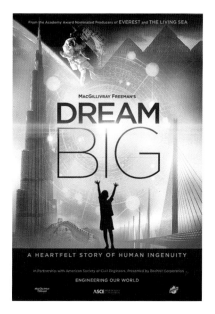

When I said at the beginning of the last chapter that "the uber-elite, mega-wealthy, black-magic-lovin' maniacal geniuses who have methodically constructed The Most Powerful City on Earth over the past two centuries went absolutely bananas with encoded symbols in this extremely-important geographic location," you now know that I wasn't exaggerating in the least.

And when I wrote, "I'm not talking about an inverted pentagram here or there," that wasn't to imply that there's not an inverted pentagram in the street layout. Indeed, there is at least one, and its tip points directly at the White House.

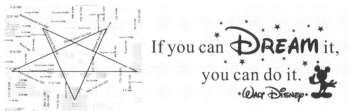

(Left) Do a Google image search for "hidden symbols in Washington, D.C." and this, or one just like it, is probably the first image that will appear.

Further, you probably thought, or hoped, that I was joking when I said that the Great Pyramid of Giza isn't the largest object encoded into the landscape. Well, I wasn't.

Welcome to "As above, so below," on crack.

MONDO MICRO-MACRO

First, I'm going to show you this:

KNIGHT OF THE SUN OR PRINCE ADEPT

THE TWENTY-EIGHTH GRADE OF THE ANCIENT AND ACCEPTED SCOTTISH RITE, AND THE TENTH DEGREE OF THE HISTORICAL AND PHILOSOPHICAL SERIES.

(Right) The apron for the Twenty-Eighth Degree features, simply, the pentagram.

Then, I'm going to show you this:

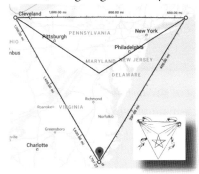

(Right) Thanks, Warren, we got it the first time.

Now, I could probably end the chapter here and everybody would have gotten the general idea, but I'm not going to.

MAKING A POINT

The tip of the smaller triangle in the image above is, of course, centered on Washington, D.C. The three points of the larger triangle are located at, pay attention:

1. Cedar Point, Rhode Island (near Jamestown);

2. Cedar Point, North Carolina; and,

3. Cedar Point, Ohio (formerly Cedar Point peninsula and now an amusement park – the, no joking, "Roller Coaster Capital of the World").

(Far right) Französischer Meister, 1675: "Der Bau der Arche Noah"

What's the point with the three Cedar Points? In a *General History and Cyclopedia of Freemasonry*, Robert MaCoy writes,

> KNIGHT OF THE ROYAL AXE, or Prince of Libanus. The 22d degree of the Ancient and Accepted rite. The legend of this degree informs us that it was instituted to record the memorable services rendered to Masonry by the mighty cedars of Lebanon, as the Sidonian architects cut down the cedars for the construction of Noah's ark.

Noah's ark? That's good enough for me. There's also some cedar-evergreen-eternity thing in Freemasonry, but we're gonna go with the ark.

Okay, we understand why the name Cedar Point was used in triplicate, but what was the overall purpose here? To encode a super-sized Masonic apron in the landscape? Big pentagram, little pentagram, As above, so below? But the larger pentagram itself isn't encoded in the landscape.

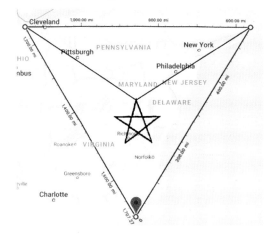

RHODES SCHOLARSHIP

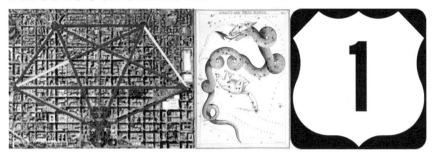

A Google image search for "hidden symbols in Washington, D.C." will very likely produce the image above left, as well, which correctly shows that the city streets also form a pentagon around the pentagram. The yellow lines segments indicate non-existent sections of road. (Remember the rules from the last chapter – that's allowed.)

The missing line segment on the left side of the inverted pentagram is aligned with Rhode Island Avenue, which points in the direction of, imagine this, the state of Rhode Island (and, perhaps even more specifically, towards Cedar Point, RI).

Interestingly, Rhode Island Avenue merges for approximately four miles in D.C. with U.S. Route 1, which subsequently continues northeast and eventually passes *within less than five miles* of Cedar Point, RI. (An item of interest here that I have not previously pointed out is that in the Upper-Half-of-D.C.-as-Great-Pyramid-of-Giza scheme, Rhode Island Avenue corresponds to the northern shaft of the King's Chamber.[1] In antiquity, this shaft pointed toward *Alpha Draconis*, a star in the constellation of *Draco*, the Dragon.)

What's all this about? The Roman-Catholic Sovereign Military Hospitaller Order of Saint John of Jerusalem of Rhodes and of Malta, also known as the Knights Hospitaller, is the oldest of the three great orders of crusading knights, the Knights Templar and the Teutonic Knights being the other two.

Following the reconquest of the Holy Land by Islamic forces, the Knights Hospitaller were based on the island of Rhodes, there becoming known as the Knights of Rhodes, and, later, on the island of Malta, thereafter being referred to as the Knights of Malta. (The Freemasonic Knight

---

1. I checked to see whether or not Massachusetts Avenue NE, which corresponds to the southern shaft of the Queen's Chamber – that, in antiquity, pointed to Sirius – is aimed at Cedar Point, Ohio. Not so much. It's pointed in that general direction … close, but no cigar. I suppose no one wanted to run the risk equating the Dog Star with an amusement park. (I *know* that the rollercoasters weren't there back when all this was put in place. Lighten up.)

of Malta Degree is known variously as the Order of Malta, or the Order of Knights of Malta, or the Ancient and Masonic Order of St John of Jerusalem, Palestine, Rhodes, and Malta.)

***

Caspar Gutman: *What do you know, sir, about the Order of the Hospital of Saint John of Jerusalem, later known as the Knights of Rhodes and other things?*

Sam Spade: *Crusaders or something, weren't they?*

– The Maltese Falcon

***

(Far Left) Rhodes was famous worldwide for the Colossus of Rhodes, one of the Seven Wonders of the Ancient World. (Left) "The New Colossus." (Right) Stained glass window depicting a Knights Hospitaller in the Church of St Andrew. (Far Right) Play it again…wrong movie.

Fine, another history lesson. Back to the matter at hand: the White House Inverted Pentagram (W.H.I.P.), whose southern tip sits on top of the White House, also points towards the super-triangle's northeastern corner in Rhode Island? In the image below, the W.H.I.P. *does* look like some monstrous device, perhaps some Magick Machine used to bind the heavens and earth together, to project that which is above onto the landscape below, unifying the Macro and the Micro.

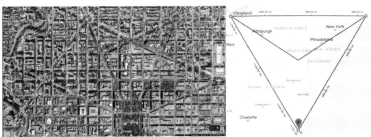

And that's an interesting thought, actually, because there's an easy trick, employing rudimentary geometry, that one can utilize to produce an inverted pentagram-pentagon at the heart of our Mega-Masonic Apron – one that is of *exactly* the same proportions as that found in the D.C. landscape directly above the White House.

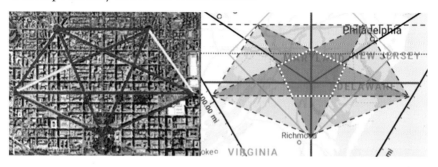

Here's how it's done.

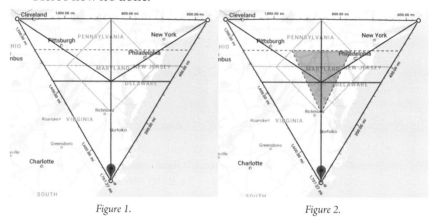

Figure 1.   Figure 2.

Figure 1:

1. Draw a cross (solid red lines) centered on the tip of the internal triangle.

2. Divide the upper portion of the large triangle in half (dashed red line).

3. Divide the bottom half of that section in half (dotted red line).

4. Washington, D.C. is at the center of the cross, and, as we know, the D.C. 10-mile square is tilted 45 degrees. Draw a tilted square (shown in light blue) centered on the dotted red line that touches the north side of the large triangle.

Figure 2:

> Construct a triangle (shown in blue) whose vertices are located: at
> the two intersections of the square and the dashed red line; and, at
> the square's southern corner. The vertices of this triangle will serve
> as three of the five vertices of the inverted pentagon, and the base
> of the triangle will serve as the pentagon's base.

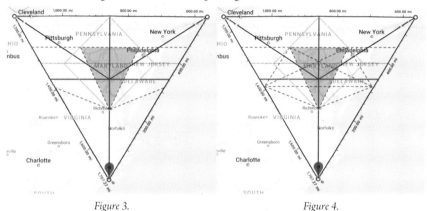

Figure 3.   Figure 4.

Figure 3:

> The length of the base of the pentagon will be the length of the two
> sides (indicated by dashed red lines) of the pentagon originating
> from its southern tip. The points where these two sides touch the
> larger triangle (in black) will be the locations of the last two verti-
> ces of the inverted pentagon.

Figure 4:

> We now have all five points of the pentagon, which are also the five
> points needed to construct the inverted pentagram. Connect the dots.

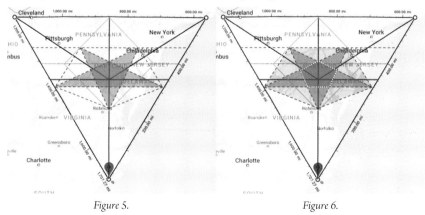

Figure 5.   Figure 6.

155

<u>Figure 5</u>:

> Inverted pentagram shown in blue. Note the internal pentagon formed at the center of the pentagram.

<u>Figure 6</u>:

> Inverted pentagon shown in light blue; internal pentagon high-lighted with dotted white line.

See, it's as easy at 1-2-3 (and 4-5-6)! (There's probably a way to do all this using angles, but I don't like angles.)

To recap, then, what we end up with is this:

As above,

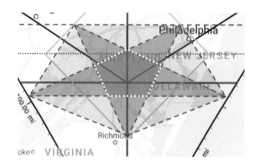

So below.

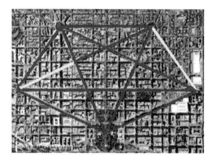

So, now you know what the purpose of the Super-Size Masonic Apron is. Any questions?

CHAPTER TWENTY-NINE

In the Beginning

S acred geometry has served as the basis for, and been incorporated into, the layouts and designs of many great cities and buildings, perhaps most notably, with regard to the latter category, gothic cathedrals. (Some researchers further assert that some cathedrals also encode Precessional Wisdom, but I don't want to talk about that.)

Pi, Phi (the golden ratio or the Golden Rule or something) and all sorts of other significant mathematical relationships are purported to have been purposely encoded into everything from the Great Pyramid to the Temple of Solomon.

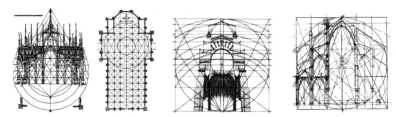

https://digital.kenyon.edu/cgi/viewcontent.cgi?referer=https://www.google.com/&httpsredir=1&article=1061&context=perejournal

To which I can only say, quoting John Cleese as Basil Fawlty in BBC's comedy series *Fawlty Towers*, "Oh Joy! Oh, thank you, God. Isn't it wonderful? I'm so happy! Hooray!"

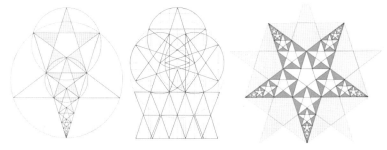

Some might say that we've already explored, at least, in part the sacred geometry of Washington, D.C., and, technically, perhaps they'd be correct, although I'm not sure I could agree with the use of the word "sacred" in this instance.

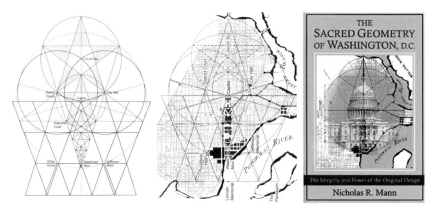

In any case, there are those who do claim that sacred geometry is the basis of the street layout of Washington, D.C., and perhaps some of them are right, or partially so. Entire volumes have been written on the subject, and we shall not explore it much further here, except to note that this topic, too, is a slippery slope and can easily end up in a place that most would consider to be utter insanity.

By way of illustration, I provide here a few images from the book pictured above, and, not being an expert in the subject and therefore not necessarily qualified to offer comment, will merely observe that if this author is by some remote chance correct in his analysis, I simply don't care enough to try to understand what in the hell is being shown here.

FROM THE START

The layout of the Washington, D.C., was designed by French-American military engineer Pierre Charles L'Enfant, and is commonly referred to as the L'Enfant Plan (completed 1791).

Following the Revolutionary War, L'Enfant established a successful engineering firm in New York City, where he was initiated into Freemasonry in 1789. Two years later, L'Enfant was appointed by fellow Freemason President George Washington to plan the new "Federal City."

(Left) Pierre Charles L'Enfant. (Right) The L'Enfant Plan.

L'Enfant was ostensibly to undertake this task under the supervision of three Commissioners also appointed by Washington, but L'Enfant insisted on full and independent authority in the design process, a demand which ultimately led to his disassociation from the project before its completion (although the plan itself was largely finished at the time).

American surveyor Andrew Ellicott, who surveyed the boundaries of the District of Columbia, was subsequently asked to complete L'Enfant's plan, and Ellicott's finished design varied little from L'Enfant's.

(Left) A 1792 print of Ellicott's "Plan of the City of Washington in the Territory of Columbia." (Right) Andrew Ellicott.

Double Cross

At this point in the book, I've either established a modicum of credibility with you, and you've continued reading out of a desire to learn more, or, you think I'm absolutely insane and you've continued reading merely to see what outrageous crap I'll spout out next (a third alternative would be a combination of the first two).

Hopefully, the former is the case, and you'll afford me a little leeway here, because I'm not going into a lot of detail on this next subject (although you know full well that I could). To put the following matter in perspective, we've talked about a lot of things, and this won't be the most surprising by any means.

The purpose of this section is to reinforce the point that everything we've been uncovering – if you had any doubts – goes way back, back to the very beginning of our country (and beyond). I've meticulously mapped this out and analyzed it with a critical eye, and I have a high degree of confidence that what I'm reporting here is accurate.

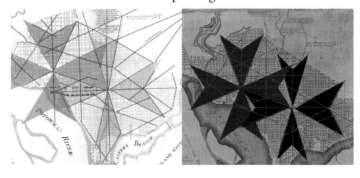

I didn't create these maps as refined graphics perfected for publication – I'm showing them so that you can see I did my homework. They're good enough to get the point across.

Included in L'Enfant's original plan for Washington, D.C., above left, (and obviously retained in Ellicott's version, above right), are two giant overlapping Maltese Crosses, one centered on the White House and the other on the U.S. Capitol Building.

I verified my findings by replicating them on a modern map of D.C.

Recalling our visual-language rules, in particular the directive to avoid making something too damn obvious – and keeping in mind that, on some level, most everything is a game to these people – I'll note a few things that are rather obvious once you begin to look at all this more closely.

The first is that there are not two *complete* Maltese Crosses present, and certainly not all of the line segments necessary to construct the shapes are found in the streetscape. I hope to God that I don't need to point out that this is because if they were complete, anybody could see them, and the gig would be up, wouldn't it? The second thing I'll note is that some of the elements are slightly distorted (or are of slightly different proportions when compared to each other), again for the same reason.

It is unclear whether Ellicott intentionally retained the crosses in his revised version of L'Enfant's plan: of the few changes he made, some of them served to enhance the cross designs (making the associated shapes more symmetrical, for instance), while others eliminated minor contributing elements. Specifically, with regard to the last point, in L'Enfant's plan there are several very short, oddly-placed streets that appear to serve no other purpose than being guidelines indicating the dimensions of the cross; these were subsequently removed by Ellicott.[1]

REINFORCING THE CENTRAL MESSAGE

If you buy all this, I would caution against interpreting these crosses as "claims of authorship or ownership." If, as I believe I have effectively shown, the two Maltese Crosses are indeed present in the streetscape of

1. For the two of you (and that estimate might be two too many) who are interested enough in this topic to actually want to hear further details, contact my publisher and he'll put you in touch with me.

Washington, D.C., this does not mean that the Knights of Malta secretly founded the United States or today run everything from behind the scenes.

We obviously know the deeper reasons why the White House and U.S. Capitol Building would be so prominently highlighted through the use of huge symbols in the layout of the city. These two massive crosses certainly reinforce the Great Cross meme in a powerful way, and each of the crosses might also be viewed as four arrow points inwardly pointing to these two extremely important physical locations.

But then there's always this much simpler explanation for why those who rule our world do these sorts of things, which is, of course, *Because they can.*

The Tools of Masonry

In addition to the House of the Temple in Washington, D.C., and the George Washington Masonic Memorial in nearby Alexandria, our nation's capital boasts 36 lodges of the Grand Lodge of Free and Accepted Masons.

As discussed earlier in this chapter, America's Premiere Freemason, George Washington, commissioned fellow Freemason, Pierre Charles L'Enfant, to design Washington, D.C.

Freemasons were also involved in the design of many of the major buildings and monuments in D.C., including:

- architect James Hoban, who designed the White House;

- Benjamin Latrobe, architect of the U.S. Capitol; and,

- Robert Mills, student of James Hoban and designer of the Washington Monument.

Further, Freemasons laid a cornerstone in most, if not all, of the major buildings in Washington, including the National Cathedral, the first Smithsonian building and the Department of Commerce/Herbert C. Hoover Building.

> *Come let me lead thee o'er this second Rome*
> *This embryo capital, where Fancy sees*
> *Squares in morasses, obelisks in trees;*
> *which second-sighted seers, ev'n now, adorn,*
> *with shrines unbuilt and heros yet unborn.*
> – "To Thomas Hume, from the City of Washington" by Thomas Moore

CHAPTER THIRTY

MACHINERY OF DEATH

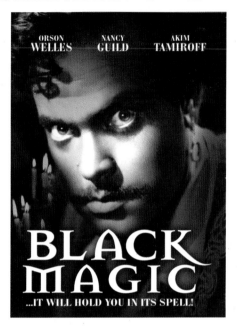

A fter all is said and done, then, perhaps what we end up with at the heart of our nation's capital is not some silly "Time Machine" as I suggested earlier, but, in fact, something far more diabolical: a Gigantic, Black-Magickal Spell-Casting Machine that incorporates all aspects of occult practice – astrology, numerology, ritual magic, device magic, astrology, numerology, blood magic and who knows what the hell else. Layer upon layer, the more ingredients, the more efficacious the spell.

(Far Right) Sigil Of Lilith

The Pentagon, inverted pentagram, obelisk, astronomical encodings, alchemical symbols – all functioning together over centuries to weave a monstrous spell, cast upon the entire world in perhaps the largest and longest mass ritual in history. And who could really argue that the whole planet is *not*, and has not been for decades, controlled from this place? (I know, we have to include the City of London and the Vatican as co-control centers.)

From the White House to the Pentagon to the U.S. Capitol to the Federal Reserve, the decisions made and actions taken in this place affect practically all of humanity. Rivers of blood are spilled upon the command of our leaders in endless military engagements and, regardless of how you feel about the issue, the millions of abortions funded by taxpayer dollars at home and abroad.

GAINING MOMENTUM

Increasingly, what we are confronted with is a combination of black-magic-on-steroids and high technology, and some would even argue metaphysical technology – a combination of *Harry Potter* and *The Matrix*.

Ever-more-sophisticated and brutal psychological warfare, combined with a multigenerational campaign of full-spectrum dominance impacting every aspect of our lives, is being waged against the American public and the global populace by our masters. It feels as though we are being pushed hard towards something very near, just over the horizon … in the not-so-distant future.

A new dawn is coming, whether supernaturally-empowered or not, and we know precisely when, don't we?

CHAPTER THIRTY-ONE

TRUMPED UP

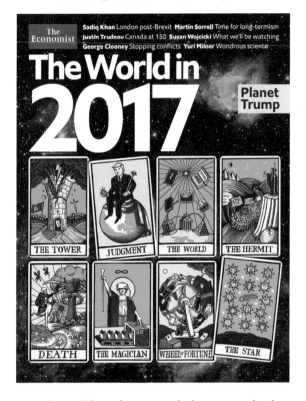

"In a moment, in the twinkling of an eye, at the last trump: for the trumpet shall sound, and the dead shall be raised incorruptible, and we shall be changed."
                                            –1 Corinthians 15:52, King James Bible

T he hour is late, and the dark spell grows blacker still. As usual, they put this right in our faces and rub our noses in it. It a sick joke, and it's on us.

WORLD-WIDE WEB

T he twenty-first Major Arcana, or trump card in the tarot deck, is The World (XXI), usually the final card in the sequence, appropriately representing the end of a cycle of life, a brief pause before the next big cycle commences.

(Left) The figure pictured at the center of The World is at once male and female, suspended between the heavens and the earth, simultaneously above and below, symbolizing completeness. (Right) A slight variation of the fifteenth trump card, The Devil.

December 21st, 2021: the 21st day of the last month of the 21st year of the 21st century. *Triple twenty-one, the End of the Great Cycle.* That which the twenty-first, and final, trump card represents is nearly upon us, and the leader of the United States and the Free World in these last days of the current great age is … Donald J. Trump.

If you don't immediately get the joke, and that it's on you (and every non-elite on the planet), there's no helping you. It's almost as obvious a nasty prank as a New York billionaire running for President as the populist savior, the Everyman's Messiah.

I mean, come on, how much more obvious can you get?

It's the year 2022...

People are still the same.

They'll do anything to get what they need.

And they need SOYLENT GREEN.

SOYLENT GREEN

MGM Presents

CHARLTON HESTON · LEIGH TAYLOR-YOUNG in SOYLENT GREEN

Co-Starring

CHUCK CONNORS · JOSEPH COTTEN · BROCK PETERS · PAULA KELLY and EDWARD G. ROBINSON

Screenplay by STANLEY R. GREENBERG · Based on a novel by HARRY HARRISON · Produced by WALTER SELTZER and RUSSELL THACHER · Directed by RICHARD FLEISCHER

PG PARENTAL GUIDANCE SUGGESTED

METROCOLOR · PANAVISION®

MGM

CHAPTER THIRTY-TWO

YEAR ZERO

Much has been written concerning the predictive programming, or intentional foreshadowing, leading up to the events of September 11, 2001 – clues and hints incorporated into multiple major motion pictures, television shows, books and so on, well before 9/11.

Ah, hah!, you're thinking (recalling our discussion from the beginning of the book), *Project Blackjack! They're going to nuke us and this was the clue!* Not so fast. Project Blackjack may have been predictive programming of sorts, but it is also something altogether more profound, and we'll revisit it in the next chapter.

Well, then, how about the movie *Soylent Green*, starring Charlton Heston, the poster for which reads at the top (as you can see on the opposite page), "It's the year 2022…"? Maybe. But I think you'll find the following example much more compelling.

BIG FAT NINNY

Nine Inch Nails (NIN) is an American industrial-rock band whose lead singer, Trent Reznor, once lived and recorded in the Los Angeles home where members of the Manson Family brutally murdered actress Sharon Tate – director Roman Polanski's wife, who was eight months pregnant at the time – and four others. Reznor dubbed his home recording studio "Le Pig," a reference to the word "pig" having been written in Tate's blood on the home's front door by one of the killers. Classy guy.

Sharon Tate starred in Eye of the Devil, *in which she played a witch. Her director and co-star in* The Fearless Vampire Killers *was Roman Polanski, whom she later married.*

In 2007, NIN released a concept album, an accompaniment to their new alternate reality game of the same name, *Year Zero.*

NINE INCH NAILS: YEAR ZERO

The fictional storyline involves various events that lead to worldwide chaos, including bioterror attacks and a nuclear war between the United States and Iran.

On February 22, 2007, a teaser trailer was released on the official Year Zero website, which was in fact one of 30 different websites associated with an extensive viral marketing campaign that included so many gimmicks, giveaways and promotional stunts (such as a mock SWAT raid on an NIN-Year Zero performance) that I'm not about to list them all here.

Like *Soylent Green*, Year Zero takes place in a dystopian future, which, again as with the movie, is set in 2022 A.D. In NIN's fictional scenario, the U.S. government, in an attempt to facilitate recovery from disaster, declares 2022 to be 0000 B.A. (Born Again), Year Zero.

2022, Year Zero.

FAIR WARNING

Before I proceed, I should point out that predictive programming is different from misinformation and disinformation, of which there was also quite a lot surrounding 9/11, pre- and post-attack.

We should therefore in this situation expect to find similar instances of purposefully misleading information, and, as usual, we can count on the History Channel to provide it.

As the screenshot above shows, one of their more recent Doom Specials featured a crack-conspiracy theorist revealing to the whole world how the Washington Monument in fact encodes the year 2022 as the End of Days, Armageddon.

But wait, you the reader might say, isn't that what _you_ said earlier? Yes, basically it is, but my explanation actually made sense, unlike this gentleman's far-fetched speculation, which somehow involved the Great Pyramid and was so absurd that I found it difficult to believe that anyone would put such a theory forward in seriousness (although I do realize there are such people).

Which led to my next thought: _Hey, this is exactly the kind of nonsense the Cryptocracy puts forward in advance of one of their shindigs._ They do a partial reveal, telling us part of the truth – that the Washington Monument encodes The End – but slather it up with such absurdity that we automatically dismiss the entire idea.

They gave us fair warning, but we chose to ignore it.

ELECTRIC EYE

And then there's this, which could just be coincidence, but I kinda doubt it: **US Military Aims to Launch Cheap New 'Blackjack' Spy Satellites in 2021**

By Mike Wall, Space.com Senior Writer | August 28, 2018 07:17am ET

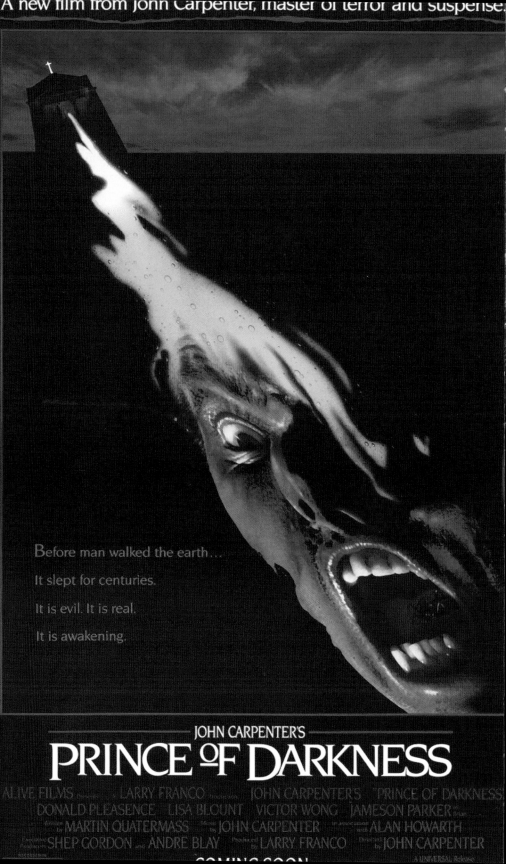

CHAPTER THIRTY-THREE

BACK TO THE BEGINNING

Here we are, almost at the end, and I'm sure most everything I'm writing at this point is starting to sound like a bunch of crap, so I'll try to wrap this up as quickly as possible.

If you haven't seen this episode of the adult comedy series South Park, *and don't know what's coming out of this character's mouth, it's not chocolate.*

We're going to finish up where we started off, with Project Blackjack. To cut to the chase, Yes, of course, the fictional scenario outlined in the slide-show would certainly, from the perspective of the Cryptocracy, constitute a fitting manner in which to greet the New Dawn of the Great Age of Satan.

Multiple nuclear detonations in the major cities of the world, hundreds of thousands dead, dying and wounded, with tens of millions more to die in the ensuing worldwide chaos and resultant global financial collapse – I mean, what's not to like?

Sounds like predictive programming to me, you say. Well, okay, if they actually go through with it, then, yes, it could be classified as predictive programming. But here's what should concern you the most.

Our friends are obliged, according to their twisted logic and occult philosophy, to provide advance warning of their intended acts of violence against us. It doesn't necessarily matter how oblique the reference, or subtle or hidden the reference, they're required to give notice.

And in this instance, we have a mysterious slideshow production, perhaps merely posing as entertainment, published on the website of one of the most prominent newspapers in the world, *thirteen* years in advance of what could be the most important event – certainly the largest potential false flag event – in all of human history.

Not only that, but the creative production presents a scenario of global catastrophe that is itself the result of a false-flag attack. This is referred to, by author Michael Hoffman, as the "Revelation of the Method," which often takes place after the fact, but there's no rule against laying everything out in the open beforehand.

Project Blackjack is a general blueprint for how a staged attack could unfold, and there are some compelling similarities between the plot of this fictitious scenario and real world circumstances – as well as several very interesting visual clues and other details.

BLUEPRINT FOR DESTRUCTION

JUNE 21 ... 2PM

JUNE 22 ... 8AM

AT A LOCK-UP GARAGE IN SOUTH EAST LONDON, A PACKAGE IS LOADED INTO A WHITE VAN

UNNOTICED ... A WHITE VAN PARKED NEAR VICTORIA, LONDON

Two slides from Project Blackjack.

New Dawn Presentations

Details from the slides, and images for comparison.

The nuclear attacks of Project Blackjack take place at the summer solstice, and are at first thought to be the work of a radical religious group, the New Dawn, but are later revealed to have been orchestrated by the global elite.

In reality, we have an approaching winter solstice, December 21st, 2021, that will mark the end of the current Great Age, and set the stage for the Dawn of the New Great Age of Satan.

Solstice. Check. New Dawn. Check.

Two additional slides from Project Blackjack: "THE BIGGEST LIE IN THE HISTORY OF THE WORLD."

At first glance, the slide on the right, above, appears to be simply showing long lines at the gas station, but upon closer examination contains some rather interesting images.

On the exterior wall of the station, where two print advertisements might have been located, are a couple of images, shown below.

Since it's so blurry, I'll give you a little help deciphering the image in the middle …

Atum, the Great He-She?

…the text below which reads, "ANNUIT COEPTIS," or "CŒPTIS," (a phrase you'll recognize from the Great Seal of the United States and translates "favor our undertakings"). The image on the right is, obviously, an inverted pentagon, with "MAJIC 12" written below it.

Annuit cœptis can be traced to a line by the Roman poet Virgil, in the *Aeneid*, book IX, line 625, which reads, *Iuppiter omnipotens, audacibus adnue coeptis*. It is a prayer offered by the son of the hero of the story, which translates to, "Jupiter Almighty, favour [my] bold undertakings."

Majic 12 (also referred to as MJ 12, Majestic 12 and several other names) was an alleged secret group of government officials, military personnel and scientists supposedly convened by President Harry Truman in 1947 to investigate UFO sightings, but whose true purpose may have been altogether different.

HIDDEN HAND

There are various other symbols, details and plot elements incorporated into the slideshow, but, in the end, an astute observer and student of the occult is left with the impression that these obscure clues are not as much neat little details snuck in by the creators of some creative viral marketing campaign as they are hints that there's a deeper purpose to this and a hidden, guiding hand behind it all.

In fact, if I am correct about whom I suspect ultimately orchestrated Project Blackjack, they may have told us as much. Included on one of the slides on an ID card is the alphanumeric sequence 74686973206973206e6f742073696d706c7920656e7465727461696e656e74. If you type this into a hexadecimal-to-string converter, it produces the following message: "This is not simply entertainment."

Those are some interesting tattoos you got there, Jason.

ountry music singer Jason Aldean, pictured above, was on stage at the Route 91 Harvest Festival in Las Vegas on October 1, 2017, when an alleged lone gunman opened fire on a crowd of approximately 22,000 people, in what turned out to be the deadliest mass shooting by an individual in U.S. history. Aldean, who ran off stage without saying a word, was unharmed.

Situated in Las Vegas, the "Gambling Capital of the World," the Las Vegas Strip, which includes the huge black, pyramid-shaped Luxor Hotel – sitting directly across from the vacant lot where the mass shooting occurred – is located largely within the unincorporated town of Paradise … which reminds me that George W. Bush was in Paradise, Florida, on the morning of 9/11, but that's a whole different story. (And God bless the folks in Paradise, California, who suffered as a result of the Camp Fire.)

Blackjack, anyone?

BACK IN BLACK

No, that's Jack Black.

Speaking of Mr. Blackjack (referencing the title of the sidebar), and recalling one last time that we are indeed on the cusp of the Dawning of the New Great Age of Satan, let's talk nicknames for a moment.

We've looked at a variety of instances of crafty meme-making, and it would just put the icing on the cake if somehow we could wrap up everything we've been contemplating into one nice memetic package and put a big fat bow on top.

And, indeed, the Cryptocracy has already done this for us, with the Ultimate in Meme-Making. How so? Recall from a previous chapter that December 21st, 2021 – The End of the current Great Age – is Triple Twenty-one: the 21st day of the last month of the 21st year of the 21st century.

The card game Blackjack is, of course, also known as Twenty-One, but it gets even better. An old nickname for our Guest of Honor, The Prince of Darkness himself? Black. Jack.

APPENDIX A:

I provide these mathematical facts essentially without comment, for they need none:

ITEM ONE: THE NAME OF GOD AND THE CYCLES OF TIME

Lord = YHWH, the Tetragrammaton, the four-letter name of God in the Judeo-Christian tradition.

- Through gematria, YHWH = 26

- Y = 10, H = 5, W = 6

- 10 + 5 + 6 + 5 = 26

- 10 + 5 = 15 + 6 = 21 + 5 = 26

- 10, 15, 21, 26

- 10 + 15 + 21 + 26 = 72 (research the 72-letter name of God)

- $10 \div 15 \div 21 \div 26 = 0.001221001221001221\ldots$

The Tetragrammaton encodes repeating cycles of 1221.

ITEM TWO: TRIPLE 21, AGAIN

The Great Age is 26,000 prophetic years – and 25,641 Illuminati years – in length, and the number of YHWH is 26.

- 26 x 25,641 = 666,666

- 666,666 ÷ pi (using 22/7) = 212121

Triple 21. Again.

ITEM THREE: FULL CIRCLE

R. ecall that 25,641 = 1221 x 21 *and* 25,641 = 777 x 33.

- Therefore, 1221 x 21 = 777 x 33, and

- 1221 / 777 = 33 / 21

Again, using 22/7 for pi, 1221/777 and 33/21 are both equal to pi/2. Half a pi and half a pi equal a whole pi. The numbers that define the Great Cycle contain a message: pi, circle, the completion of one full cycle – *we have come FULL CIRCLE.*

APPENDIX B:

I provide these images with comment, although they need none:

(Left) I don't care who you are or what your little religion says, there's no excuse for this, ever. (Right) Or this.

(Left) Monsters, Inc. (Right) Monsters, Inc., the Prequel (Clinton, Bush and George Wallace)